DATE DUE

DEMCO INC 38-2971

FADED MOSAIC

Christopher Clausen

FADED MOSAIC

THE EMERGENCE OF POST-CULTURAL AMERICA

Ivan R. Dee

CHICAGO 2000

Library of Congress Cataloging-in-Publication Data:
Clausen, Christopher, 1942–
    Faded mosaic : the emergence of post-cultural America /
Christopher Clausen.
        p. cm.
    Includes bibliographical references and index.
    ISBN 1-56663-283-8 (alk. paper)
        1. United States—Civilization—1945– 2. Pluralism (Social sciences)—United States. 3. Multiculturalism—United States.
4. Culture—Philosophy. 5. Culture—Social aspects—United States.
6. Culture conflict—United States. 7. United States—Ethnic relations. 8. United States—Social conditions—1980– 9. National characteristics, American. 10. Assimilation (Sociology). I. Title.

E169.12.C543 2000
306'.0973—dc21   99-059433

for
Marjorie and John Hunt

Acknowledgments

This book had its origins in an essay entitled "Welcome to Post-Culturalism," which appeared in the *American Scholar* for Summer 1996. I thank Joseph Epstein for advice on the essay and, when it began to look like a book, for recommending Ivan Dee to me. Part of Chapter 2 originally appeared in *Queen's Quarterly* (Canada) for Summer 1999 under the title "Nostalgia, Freedom, and the End of Cultures."

A number of people have read and commented on all or parts of the manuscript. Among them are Bernard Asbell, who gave generous help and advice; Dr. Everett Dulit and his psychiatric colleagues at Montefiore Medical Center, New York, where I delivered the 1998 Ed Hornick Memorial

Acknowledgments

Lecture on the subject of post-culturalism; Peter Graham of Virginia Polytechnic Institute and State University; Peter Nicolaisen, a German scholar of American life and literature, from whom I have learned more about America than I ever expected; and most of all Nancy Clausen, whose assistance, as always, has been indispensable at every stage. I thank all of them for their generosity. Whatever follies and delusions remain are my own. I also thank The Pennsylvania State University for sabbatical leave that enabled me to concentrate my attention on large issues.

Sean Grass, my resourceful and indefatigable research assistant, resurrected large bodies of demographic fact and figure from the library and the Internet while simultaneously completing a dissertation on a different set of social concerns in the Victorian novel. The incongruity of the two projects never seemed to faze him.

My father, John A. Clausen, was a sociologist who spent his later years studying changes in American lives between the 1930s and the 1990s. There is no telling how much of this book he would have approved of, but whatever is good in it must owe something to a youth passed in the company of distinguished social scientists.

Contents

Mr. Lincoln was telling his countrymen that the achieved West had given the United States something that no people had ever had before, an internal, domestic empire, and he was telling them that Yesterday must not be permitted to Balkanize it.

—Bernard DeVoto, *The Year of Decision: 1846* (1943)

On those streets was America, all of it different but all of it the same, going to work and to school, sewing clothes and shopping for food, praying and bowling and reading and worrying, minding its children and mowing the lawn, washing, hoping, running the bases, living, dying, and in love in between, a tribe made up of many tribes, strewn from sea to shining sea. . . . There was room under the sky for all of it, and if someday there was no more room, then America would build a bigger sky.

—Ev Ehrlich, *Big Government* (1998)

FADED MOSAIC

Introduction

Freedom and Nostalgia

What kind of culture, or "mosaic" of cultures, is the United States of America at the start of the third millennium, and what difference does it make to the people who live here? Or to the rest of the world? In one form or another, these have become common, even compulsive questions. Almost everyone agrees that America is not the same country it was half a century ago. There is much less consensus on the nature of the changes, and hardly any on whether they have been mainly for better or worse.

In 1957, the year of Sputnik and the Little Rock school desegregation riots, Max Lerner, then a well-known historian, journalist, and liberal polemicist, published a massive volume called *America as a Civilization*. His book, which attracted widespread acclaim, was partly history, partly anthropology, partly a study of attitudes as they had evolved over the centuries since the first European colonists arrived. The main focus, however, was on the United States in the middle of the twentieth century. The book's thesis was explicit in its title. "For good or ill," Lerner explained early in his thousand pages, "America is what it is—a culture in its own right, with many characteristic lines of power and meaning of its own, ranking with Greece and Rome as one of the great distinctive civilizations of history."[1]

Lerner was well aware that the terms *culture* and *civilization* had well-established scholarly meanings, and he defined them carefully for his purposes. What he called "the culture concept" was "largely derived from the anthropologists who discovered that every people, no matter how primitive, had an organic culture. . . . What emerged from their work, and especially from that of Ruth Benedict and Margaret Mead, was the key idea that cultures are organic patterns to be treated as living wholes." Applying this concept of culture to the United States seemed to Lerner a straightforward task:

> America is at once *culture* and *civilization*, and *society* as well. The terms refer to different aspects of the same whole rather than to different segments of it. "Culture" . . . has become the key term of the social sciences. I use it to mean the *matrix* of American living, the stuff of life that is transmitted, learned, and relearned, with the stress on the "designs for living"—the

norms and beliefs and all the curious and twisted shapes they take. . . . "Society" refers to the total group and institutional framework, and the processes of living together and being knit together within it as *socii* or members of the same commonalty.

Civilization, on the other hand, was something special, more important than an average, run-of-the-mill culture or society. "When a culture . . . has grown highly complex and has cut a wide swath in history and in the minds of men, one looks for a term more highly charged with the overtones of these meanings. 'Civilization' is such a term." For Lerner the word conjured up not only Greece and Rome but China and Britain, Renaissance Italy and Aztec Mexico, Russia and, of course, America. All its past and present flaws notwithstanding, the United States would be seen by future historians as "one of the memorable civilizations of history," in large part because it united such a rich mixture of ingredients.

Although Lerner rejected the conformist implications of the already venerable "melting pot" image, he had no doubt that American civilization was a suspension of elements from different times and places. Immigrants had not simply abandoned their original identities at Plymouth Rock or Ellis Island; the making of America was a dynamic process that transformed everyone: "Unless those identities were changed and dissolved in the process, shaped and reshaped, caught up in the ever-flowing stream of the life of all of them together, it would be meaningless to talk of America." Summarizing the already well-established doctrine known as liberal pluralism, he added, "The problem for the recent newcomers and their children, as indeed for all Americans, is to hold several cultures in organic suspension, weaving each in with the other in a process without which American society as we know it could not have been formed." Old-style assimilation ("a one-way drive") was out, replaced by integration ("a two-way circuit").

Less than half a century later, Lerner's book looks as ancient as the Pyramids in its confidence, its assumptions, and even its style. It now seems paradoxical that in 1957, the year when Soviet technological prowess abroad and the intractability of racial inequality at home emerged as inescapable facts of life, few Americans of any political persuasion doubted the worth—to themselves and to the rest of the world—of their national ideals and institutions. At the turn of the millennium, by contrast, with legalized segregation and the Soviet Union both distant memories, Americans sitting on top of the world seemed far less sure of themselves as a nation or, in Lerner's terms, a civilization.

One of the things they learned to doubt in the intervening decades was whether one country had much of value to teach another, a lesson that cast doubt on America's de facto position as world leader and democratic model. Another, closely related doubt had to do with the question of whether the United States was still—or in fact had ever been—a single country or civilization, as opposed to a Babel of more or less mutually incomprehensible cultures. It has, in fact, become something of a cliché in recent years that Americans no longer possess a common culture. Rather, as

Andrew Sullivan put it in the *New York Times Magazine* for November 15, 1998, "as subcultures have replaced a national culture," we have become more diverse, pluralistic, fragmented, multicultural, or whatever word happens to be currently in vogue.

This assertion may be correct, but not quite in the sense that Sullivan intended. So far as exerting decisive power over its members as traditional cultures used to do—dictating directions and setting limitations on thoughts or behavior—it is true that America no longer has a single, dominant culture. But at the same time most of its subcultures, or ancestral cultures, are not in very potent shape either. Apart from the survival of the English language, this loss of distinctiveness and confidence applies just as much to the WASP-derived dominant American culture of the nineteenth century as to contemporary immigrant cultures from outside Europe. Twentieth-century America has in fact been an expanding graveyard of cultures.

Amid a profusion of books and articles on multiculturalism in American society, this historically unprecedented situation has scarcely been noticed. One familiar school of thought—loosely described as liberal or radical—holds with Sullivan that as the concept of a majority culture has broken down, the cultures of ethnic and other minorities (some of them recent immigrants) have been coming back into their own after centuries of suppression. A nearly opposite point of view—loosely described as conservative—maintains that immigrants and their descendants, regardless of ethnicity, have been assimilating more rapidly than ever to what Lerner described as American civilization, and would do so in even greater numbers were it not for public policies that encourage the revival of old identities. The argument of this book is that both "liberals" and "conservatives" are factually mistaken. Although one emphasizes diversity and the other unity, they both cling to a notion of real cultures that is now obsolete. In striking contrast to societies of the past, the contemporary United States has neither one big culture nor a number of smaller ones, only a strange mixture of freedom and nostalgia.

This situation requires a less misleading name than multiculturalism. With apologies for introducing another neologism beginning with *post*, I call it post-culturalism. As a label, the word at least has the virtue of saying what it means.[2] Contemporary America is the first post-cultural society, a society existing after the death of cultures.

With few exceptions, the most significant dividing lines among Americans today are age and income, not ancestral origins or even region of residence. Being of Italian or Polish or Jewish descent no longer offers much predictive value about the shape a person's life will take. Nor does being Hispanic or Arab American. Being a Hopi Indian is another matter, but only as long as one lives on a reservation and associates primarily with other Hopis. Being black, or African American, is also an exception, though to a diminishing extent. But despite the fact that in careless moments multiculturalists treat culture and race as if they were synonyms, blackness is a color, not a culture. ("Although Britain has a multi-cultural society," a writer for the London *Daily Telegraph* demanded on July 20, 1973, "where are the black faces among television announcers, newscasters, and commentators?") If it were not immediately visible, the power of African descent over the lives of those who possess it would have vanished long ago, together with their "cultural" distinctiveness from the majority.

Nathan Glazer, a distinguished social commentator who had been one of the strongest supporters of liberal pluralism—residual ethnic identities within the context of a universal American culture—seemed to change sides in 1997 with a book aggressively entitled *We Are All Multiculturalists Now.* His explicit basis for doing so was the failure of the normal assimilation process, in either its melting-pot or pluralist phases, to include black Americans. Only that inclusion, he declared in his last sentence, would "reduce multiculturalism to a passing phase in the complex history of the making of an American nation from many strands."[3] For Glazer, persisting divisions between black and white Americans are the only persuasive rationale for the government and educational policies that have come to be described as multicultural and are the only important, long-lasting challenge to the efficacy of assimilation.

Even so, by any realistic standard, Americans of all races on the doormat of the third millennium have far more in common than they did when Max Lerner was writing, or than it is now fashionable to recognize. This convergence is neither all good nor all bad, but in spite of frequent heated denials it is a fact. Consider for a moment the media of entertainment and education that affect everyone. For the most part Americans do not read the same books (in many cases any books at all) or even watch the same television channels. On the other hand, to cite survey data that are less trivial than they seem, Americans of all races spend more time between birth and death watching television than in any other activity except working and sleeping, ranging from a weekly average of more than twenty-two hours for small children to more than forty-one hours for women over fifty-five.[4]

The difference between watching television and not watching it—the difference in how one is looking at, relating to, understanding the world or oneself—is, as Marshall McLuhan pointed out in the 1960s, qualitatively more important than the difference between any two channels. A presidential campaign, a hurricane, and the funeral of a princess may have more in common as television experiences than any one of them has with a newspaper account of the same event. The increasing use of computers as primary media of information and communication imposes even greater similarities of attitude.

As for our public educational system, where otherness long ago replaced motherhood as the official piety-in-chief, the fact that it no longer stresses a detailed grounding in, or in many respects a positive view of, American history and institutions disguises the fact that in the past thirty years it has become more uniform than ever. From Hyannis to Honolulu, American schools celebrate diversity with a minimum of local variation. Universities too, both public and private, have become far more alike than they were in the days when each kind of institution catered to an identifiable ethnic, religious, or regional population of prospective students. Competing today for the same students, faculty members, research grants, and appropriations, in the very process of emphasizing cultural differences they become ever more similar.

Here as in other areas of life, a lot depends on what you mean by the word *culture*. Lerner's careful application of the term has become a thing of the past. In journalistic and often in scholarly usage, every government agency or large corporation now has its own "culture." Sex scandals in the army, navy, and air force are casually attributed to the culture of the armed forces; the culture of political campaigns leads to endemic corruption and should be reformed; the increasingly pervasive Internet is often described as a culture; and so on. In contrast to these micro-referents, the same term is routinely applied to a large and venerable entity called Western culture.

What exactly do open-minded vacationers mean when they speak of "learning another culture" as a by-product of a Mediterranean or South American cruise? Or, more ominously, when commentators declare that "the culture" is responsible for violence in schools? The fact that the word is now used so loosely, to label such a wide array of real and imaginary entities, suggests that few of the people who use it have much conception of what real cultures are, or were. For many who speak confidently about "culture," the term serves not to explain anything but to conceal the lack of an answer for whatever question is being asked. The point here is not to ridicule thoughtless usage, entertaining and useful though that task can sometimes be, but to explore what purposes such a watered-down and inconsistent notion of culture serves in the age of the Internet—which might seem in its openness, its lack of fixed norms, its enthusiasm for the young and the new, its lightning growth, its absence of historical associations, to be the perfect opposite of a culture.

Much larger issues are at stake here than vocabulary. First is the nature of the causes—from the printing press to the steamship to cable television—that have gone so far to break down cultural distinctiveness, not only in the United States, which after all began national life more than two centuries ago with universalistic ideas about human nature and rights, but in most of the world. As the uneven but impressive progress of those ideas beyond our shores suggests, not all the causes of what I call post-culturalism are technological, though some are.

What is the present status of cultural relativism in a society, or on a planet, where the term *culture* and the objects it supposedly denotes are more nebulous than ever before? What does it mean in the age of CNN (a network that forbids its broadcasters to use the word *foreign*) to say that one "culture" permits what another forbids? Should, for example, slavery be immune to outside criticism in places, like the central African country of Sudan, where it has existed for uncounted centuries? Few multiculturalists would go so far. Even the authoritarian governments of China and Singapore, which energetically quote Western anthropological theories to deflect criticism of human-rights abuses, concede in principle that some ethical standards are universally binding. Does the newly popular rhetoric of human rights imply that "globalization," another popular 1990s term, is leading us toward a single worldwide civilization, or to its opposite, the end of all civilizations as history has known them?

In American courts, meanwhile, what has recently come to be called the "cultural defense" argues that at least certain parts of the criminal law should not be applied to immigrants from countries where accepted behavior differs from American standards. What implications does the somewhat contradictory consensus that every culture has its own valid customs, but that some human rights are universal, have in such varied contexts as a trial for domestic violence in the Midwest or for Balkan war crimes at The Hague?

In spite of efforts to validate what remains of cultural traditions, the effects of post-culturalism are transforming American life. One important result out of many is the extreme emphasis on personal feelings and self-gratification that I explored in another context in *My Life with President Kennedy* (1994) and to which I return in Chapter 4. A usually unreflective, often sentimental, sometimes violent style of individualism gains strength when the values and inhibitions central to any traditional culture lose their authority. The emotional worldwide response to the death of Princess Diana in 1997 was, in all its shallowness, a deeply post-cultural event. So in a different way was the 1999 school massacre at Littleton, Colorado—an act of extreme violence motivated not by ancestral hatreds but by something newer, harder to pin down or combat.

By all odds the most contentious issue raised by post-culturalism has to do with formerly distinct cultural groups that have seen their identities threatened and want to preserve or restore them. In the United States this nostalgia paradoxically unites the multicultural left with the family-values right. Properly seen, it constitutes one of the salient characteristics of American cultural life, popular and elite, at the beginning of the twenty-first century. A galaxy of inflammatory social issues, from affirmative action to bilingual education all the way through the alphabet to school prayer and zero immigration, revolve in erratic orbits around the highly predictable phenomenon of culture and its loss. Elsewhere in the world, the same nostalgia has given rise to a phrase that was unknown before the 1990s: ethnic cleansing.

Two more or less peaceful North American attempts at cultural preservation, to be explored later in more detail, may offer a better idea here of what is at stake. One is the American Jewish community (*community*, like *culture*, has become a much abused word), about whose survival an enormous amount has been written in the past twenty years—with a rising sense of urgency. According to some well-attested figures, Jews in the United States now intermarry with non-Jews at a rate exceeding 50 percent. In the 1950s, when Max Lerner was writing, the rate was about 6 percent. Because relatively few American Jews today speak Yiddish or identify strongly with those aspects of Judaism that made their grandparents part of a distinctly Jewish culture, it has become hard for any but the most uncompromisingly Orthodox to find a secure basis for avoiding assimilation. It has often been pointed out that the prominence of the Holocaust in the American consciousness since the 1960s owes something to this search for a durable Jewish identity that does not depend on religious belief.

If we contrast American Jews with the French-speaking inhabitants of Quebec, we find a minority culture whose current political leadership has made resisting assimilation its highest priority and energetically uses the law to pre-serve its language. That means, among other things, out-lawing the use of English in as many public settings as possible. Is this set of policies an example of multicultural-ism (a term that seems to have originated in Canada) or its opposite? Are the separatism and hatred of outsiders that sometimes accompany such policies inextricable from any serious attempt to preserve a distinct culture today? Of course this situation differs significantly from that of Amer-ican Jews, who have no province in which they constitute a majority. Still, the Quebecois dilemma bears an irreducible resemblance to that of Jews: secede or disappear. We see similar conflicts virtually everywhere in the modern world, with outcomes ranging from assimilation to velvet divorce to genocide.

My own ambivalence about these issues will be evident at every stage. Universalism, openness, and equality are basic Enlightenment values that much of the world yearns for. At its deepest level, post-culturalism is the outgrowth of liberties that people in many countries would, and fre-quently do, die for. On the less apocalyptic level of day-to-day living in America, why should anyone be forced to choose once and for all between knishes and curry? Or, to put the advantages positively, why shouldn't we all be free to choose among as many of the earth's possibilities as exist, not only in food but in the more important realms of art, attitudes, heroes, philosophical insights, and marriage? "Assimilation" today need not mean giving up everything that came from somewhere else. In its post-cultural form it means having access to all the world's inherited intangibles.

On the other side of the coin, the freedom that lies beyond culture may be a mixed blessing. Increasingly Americans grow up in places with no identity, as in the California tract whose developer proudly explained its name in the *New York Times Magazine* (July 11, 1999): "'Ladera' doesn't mean a thing; it's value-neutral. So the residents can hang on the word the idea of what they are." But how can they know who they are or where they want to go in an environment where even the names on the map are meaningless? In reality *ladera* is a Spanish word for hillside. The builder's ignorance and the advantage he saw in a name with no meaning merely emphasize the uncertainties of post-culturalism. The streets of Ladera may well lead only to aimless narcissism, a liberty that not even John Stuart Mill could love. No wonder many parents find themselves attracted by the prospect of raising their children in planned communities like the Disney Corporation's Celebration, Florida, which imitates the appearance and "lifestyle" associated with a small Midwestern or New England town around 1900. At the same time, Norman Rockwell's paintings of an idealized small-town America have become more popular than ever.

In the absence of a culture that points directions and makes enforceable demands, my own immediate gratification threatens to become the only criterion of value. Moreover, the decline of cultural identity, though it reduces some sources of conflict, does not necessarily strengthen or liberate individuals. In many ways it confuses and impoverishes them. Of course, loss of cultural distinctiveness does not mean that forms of difference based on other factors will cease to exist; they may well increase as cultures and subcultures continue losing the capacity to impose a uniform outlook on their own members. But meanwhile much of the rich particularity in American life, its teeming variety, is replaced by market-tested counterfeits of a diversity that really belongs to the past.

This book is not about the so-called culture wars but about some of their deepest causes. It will try to examine what Americans (and to a lesser extent people in other parts of the world) really mean and are really valuing when they talk about preserving cultural diversity or traditional culture, and above all what adjustments they make in practice when a real culture ceases to guide their lives. Before we can examine the gaudy peculiarities of life in the post-cultural era, however, we need to spend a chapter looking at the history of culture—of the concept itself—as early twentieth-century anthropologists pummeled and kneaded it and, contrary to their own intentions, helped turn it into a shapeless blob. Accordingly, this book begins with a critical glance at what might be called the cultural construction of culture.

Chapter One

The Cult of
"Culture"

Writing in 1995 about the then rela-
tively unfamiliar Internet, Gary Chapman described its
adepts as "the intellectual vanguard for an internationalist,
libertarian world-view of global, amoral, stateless capitalism" and contrasted this vision with "the nativist, patriotic
'family values' apparently ascendant in the American middle
class." Chapman, director of the 21st Century Project at the
University of Texas, believed that the increasing use of computer networks had greatly strengthened the first of these
outlooks and weakened American "parochialism," a frame
of mind for which he thought "family values" was merely a
rationalization. Politicians, he maintained, had failed to

grasp either the "culture" of the Internet or its implications for the politics they practiced.

Apart from pointing out the difficulty of regulating cyberspace and emphasizing "net users' rising disdain for government . . . because regulation represents a penetration of alien and unwelcome ideas into perhaps the only domain where rules and behavior are largely disconnected from government coercion," Chapman had little to say about what the Internet's political implications might be.[1] Readers who are not "digerati" may suspect that, like other enthusiasts, he exaggerated the influence of computers on the way most people think or behave. He did, however, neatly encapsulate two frames of mind that increasingly polarize political and cultural controversy, not only in the United States but in much of the world.

On one side are libertarians, free-traders, believers in open borders, optimistic space travelers through the modern world whose lifeblood is "information" in the various senses of that protean buzzword. On the other side are a diverse aggregation of neoisolationists, nationalists, advocates of restricted trade and immigration, cultural protectionists, religious believers who demand that the state use its power to enforce traditional prohibitions against homosexuality, illegitimacy, abortion, and many forms of incivility. This latter set of positions has one conspicuous counterpart in much of the non-Western world—Muslim fundamentalism. It is *Jihad vs. McWorld,* as the political scientist Benjamin Barber memorably labeled the conflict in a laconic book title the same year Chapman was writing (though by *Jihad*

Barber meant something broader than just Islamic resistance to modernity).

My concern here is not with political controversy as such but with the unfolding cultural history it sometimes reflects. The relationship between cultural change and its expression in politics, whether electoral or intellectual, is not always what one would expect. For example, a libertarian, internationalist vision of the world should in theory be just what academic and bureaucratic advocates of "diversity" and multiculturalism have been dreaming of. On the Internet or in a world of permeable borders, where there is plenty of room for everyone and everything, different cultures should for the first time be able to flourish side by side in relationships unmarked by either dominance or submission. Internet enthusiasts like Chapman often describe the object of their devotion in just such terms, as being itself a new culture where, finally, a universal, utopian equality has been achieved.

In fact the Internet can serve as a revealing metaphor for attitudes toward culture and the ways culture has been changing in the past half-century, starting even before it was invented. For example, ignoring the fact that the same medium is frequently used to propagate messages of hatred and violence, John R. Levine, Carol Baroudi, and Margaret Levine Young proudly announce in their book *The Internet for Dummies* that the Internet is "politically, socially, and religiously correct":

> Another unusual thing about the Internet is that it is what one might call "socially unstratified." That is, one

computer is no better than any other. Who you are on the Internet depends solely on how you present yourself through your keyboard. If what you say makes you sound like an intelligent, interesting person, that's who you are. It doesn't matter how old you are or what you look like or whether you're a student, a business executive, or a construction worker. Physical disabilities don't matter—we correspond with people who are blind or deaf. . . . People become famous in the Net community, some favorably and some unfavorably, but they get that way through their own efforts.[2]

In reality, of course, money and education, the usual bases of social stratification in modern America, are at a premium in first buying the machinery and then communicating effectively over a computer network. One computer is very much better than another in this compulsively up-to-date "community." Likewise, the ability to fit in by communicating a certain set of attitudes in a certain kind of idiomatic English is essential. The authors' set of egalitarian fantasies reveals far more about their relation to and understanding of their own society than it does about the Internet. As they describe it, their desire for connectedness finds its outlet not in real human relations, or in the other common practices of real cultures, but in one of the most restricted, protocol-driven, nearly anonymous forms of human communication.

The rapid proliferation of the Internet resembles kudzu more than culture. Yet the widespread idealization of the electronic "global village" is further confirmation that for more than a century the dynamic of American life has been systematically breaking down not merely the boundaries between cultures but the real content that defines cultures and binds people to them. This process began long before computers were invented. Whether we label it modernity, liberal individualism, cultural imperialism, consumerism, the technological revolution, globalization, or the inexorable logic of capitalism, no culture is immune to it. The result is a United States, and arguably an entire world, fast approaching a condition that can best be described not as multicultural but as post-cultural.

Notice again that Chapman referred to the "culture" engendered by the Internet. As Max Lerner pointed out in 1957, the word *culture,* when used anthropologically rather than as a synonym for art and entertainment, refers to the total structure of life of a particular society. Margaret Mead, then at the height of her popularity, characterized culture in 1959 as "the systematic body of learned behavior which is transmitted from parents to children."[3] This use of the word was introduced by Sir Edward Burnett Tylor, a founder of modern anthropology, in his book *Primitive Culture* (1871): "Culture, or Civilization, taken in its wide ethnographic sense, is that complex whole which includes knowledge, belief, art, morals, law, custom, and any other capabilities and habits acquired by man as a member of society." With an enthusiastic Victorian faith in the capacity of science to illuminate the remaining obscurities of life, Tylor added, "The condition of culture among the various societies of mankind, in so far as it is capable of being investigated on general principles, is a subject apt for the study of laws of human thought and action."[4]

In the broadest anthropological sense of the word, the totality of learned behavior is "culture," and in that sense culture exists by definition in all human societies. But in traditional anthropology the word carries an additional implication that long ago entered into general circulation through the work of such popular early twentieth-century writers as Mead and Ruth Benedict. That implication accounts for much of the confusion with which the term is used today: cultural determinism, the power of a culture to dominate, even dictate the thoughts and behavior of its members. Cultural determinism, together with its supposed corollary cultural relativism—the idea that no culture is better than another—remains an entrenched academic dogma in the humanities and social sciences. It is also widely, if unreflectively, taken for granted in popular usage.

"By the time [a child] can talk," Benedict announced in her immensely influential *Patterns of Culture,* "he is the little creature of his culture, and by the time he is grown and able to take part in its activities, its habits are his habits, its beliefs his beliefs, its impossibilities his impossibilities. Every child that is born into his group will share them with him, and no child born into one on the opposite side of the globe can ever achieve the thousandth part." In case the reader should miss the point that cultures are uncompromising in their exclusiveness, Benedict emphasizes: "Outside of the closed group there are no human beings."[5] The cultures of Inca Peru or Anglo-Saxon England, for example, may have altered over time, but each had certain constant features, including a language, that differentiated it from other cultures in other times or places. A culture is defined more sharply by those differences and exclusions than by its own positive selection from "the great arc of human potentialities"—that is, not only by what it includes but above all by what it keeps out.

The "culture" of the Internet is another story altogether and requires a different kind of telling. Used in a half-consciously metaphorical sense, *culture* is everywhere these days. The latest edition of *Books in Print* contains nearly five columns in minuscule type of titles such as *The Culture of Addiction, The Culture of Biomedicine, The Culture of Childhood; of Complaint, Disbelief, Protest, Science, the University,* and *War.* A *New York Times* story of April 17, 1994, about a company that makes preppy clothes for a black clientele, paraphrased the owner, Charles Walker, Jr., to the effect that Ralph Lauren and Tommy Hilfiger "didn't make clothes that reflected blacks' lifestyles or culture." Walker's new Heritage line of "Afrocentric preppy" gear, said the *Times*, "allows the wearer both to dress in preppy style and to express cultural pride." Around the same time, the news from South Africa included a controversy about whether Zulus should be allowed to carry such "cultural weapons" as spears and machetes in political demonstrations.

Today the press is filled with stories about the "culture" of the Defense Department, the Central Intelligence Agency, Congress, and any large corporation that happens to be in the news. In 1998 Senator Daniel Patrick Moynihan, a distinguished sociologist, published a book about the "culture of secrecy" in the federal government. The *Washington Post* for January 17, 1999, quoted Michael Lenard, a former vice president of the United States Olympic Committee, as saying about the International Olympic Committee's apparently long-established habit of accepting "gifts" from cities that sought to host games: "It is not a culture of corruption, it is a culture of quid pro quo." A *New Republic* article about Bill Gates in 1998 was described on the cover as being about "the culture of Microsoft-bashing." *GQ* even described opera in 1995 as being characterized by "the culture of booing."

Culture is often associated with place, and state tourist offices use the same modish language of culture and difference with the same hopeful lack of definition. Consider a series of travel advertisements from the early 1990s, shortly after *culture* broke out of its disciplinary chains and began climbing the Empire State Building. "Visit a Country Where You Can Experience a Unique Culture," Texas advertised. "In Texas you'll find a whole other way of life. It's a place where an old iron gate is sculpted into a beautiful work of art. And something as common as a cowboy boot takes on monumental importance. Listen to music that's uniquely country. And eat barbecue that's out of this world."

In the same March–April 1992 issue of the *National Geographic Traveler*, San Francisco described the scenic resources that make it an attractive tourist destination but added, "You need three-quarters of a million very fortunate people—from every imaginable culture but united by the sheer joy of living in such a wondrous place as this." A few pages later the Canadian province of Newfoundland advertised "Natural Wonders—Intriguing Tours—Unique Culture—Fascinating History—Exquisite Cuisine," while Nevada highlighted its residents of Basque descent: "Their rugged history is European legend, but did you know that these hearty people are also part of the colorful culture of Nevada?"

What did the agencies that created these advertisements believe the word *culture* would convey, and why did they think it would attract free-spending visitors? The Texas ad associates culture with the rural past and with being a separate country, playing on the fact that Texas was briefly an independent republic. The San Francisco ad, on the other hand, assumes that a culture is something people—at least San Franciscans—are from, not in: something of another time and place left behind willingly, even joyously for the pleasure of living in such a fine city. Newfoundland juxtaposes culture with natural scenery (like San Francisco) and food (like Texas) while explicitly adding the dimension of history. (Again, culture has to do with the past.) Nevada drags in *European* history, something clearly remote from the state, and describes its own culture with the single, vague word "colorful." How different these places may be from one another in any way that can usefully be called cultural is debatable, but they all draw on the same superficial assumptions about culture to market themselves.

H as the word *culture* acquired by now the same cultural status as a cough? Yes and no. Clearly, most of the time *culture* is a lazy, trendy substitute for a more specific word. Sometimes the writer really means shared attitudes, sometimes fashion, sometimes behavior, sometimes mere local color. The concept of culture carries with it, however, two serious implications in contemporary usage, both of which derive in different ways from popular anthropology.

First, whatever is cultural is presumed not to be biologically determined, despite the frequent sloppy equation of culture with race. William Connolly reflected this implication of the word when he complained in the April 10, 1994, *New York Times Book Review* about "the cultural demand for heterosexuality." If heterosexuality is only a "cultural demand," and not a matter of biology, its normative status ranks as a mere prejudice and can be changed, as Connolly thinks it ought to be (though the ability of advocates to reverse a "cultural demand" seems to suggest that cultural determinism is not very powerful after all). In this argument he echoes Ruth Benedict, who devoted several impassioned pages to the "honorable estate" of homosexual practices in some past cultures.

How the "cultural demand" for heterosexuality arose in the first place, or why it arose so powerfully in some places but not in others, or why it has recently lost so much of its force in Europe and America, are questions beyond the range of culture-centered explanations. Culture has become a familiar whipping boy, particularly where sex is involved. "I'm no longer willing to call it an illness, the kind of promiscuity I engaged in between 1960 and 1970," Jeffrey Masson told the *Philadelphia Inquirer* (September 3, 1995). "But it was probably cultural."

On the other hand, the second serious implication of "culture" is that it can be an excuse, a rhetorical device to place some taste or practice beyond criticism. "The principle of cultural relativism," the great anthropologist Alfred Kroeber wrote in 1952, "has long been standard anthropological doctrine. It holds that any cultural phenomenon must be understood and evaluated in terms of the culture of which it forms part."[6] In other words, there is no standard beyond culture from which a particular culture's practices may be judged. The Zulus of South Africa feel that their "cultural weapons" should be exempt from bans that apply to other weapons; otherwise their culture is being discriminated against. (Some residents of the American West make the same argument about their favorite firearms but get little sympathy from the news media. Even classic Colts and Winchesters are not quite cultural yet.) "Cultural" is not being used here with the implication that carrying spears, like demanding heterosexuality, is a vestige of less enlightened times and should be discontinued. Quite the opposite. To deprive Zulus of their spears is to attack their culture. And to attack a culture these days will sooner or later inspire a charge of genocide, another growth stock on the lexical market.

Describing something as the product of culture can therefore imply either of two contradictory things about it: that it is not genetically fixed and can (usually should) be changed, or that it exists in an autonomous realm where, because of the doctrine of cultural relativism, it carries full immunity to criticism from outside. In contemporary polemics, what radical multiculturalists castigate as "Euro-centric male culture" is often attacked from the first per-spective (as a collection of prejudices to be overcome), while non-Western or minority "culture" is often defended from the second (as a precious inheritance that should be beyond criticism).

At the United Nations World Conference on Human Rights in 1993, China, Iraq, and other Asian dictatorships invoked cultural relativism to contend that Western com-plaints about their human-rights abuses represented a form of imperialism. "Universal recognition of the ideal of human rights can be harmful if universalism is used to deny or mask the reality of diversity," declared the foreign minis-ter of Singapore.[7] The forcible suppression of dissenters, the argument went, may violate European and American norms, but the ancient cultures of the East have the right to follow their own customs. In some versions of this de-fense by the Chinese and Singaporean governments, the modern police state becomes an expression of traditional Confucian morality, while in African versions the idealized village or tribe becomes the rationalization for one-party au-thoritarianism, or worse.

Besides the fact that this whole line of argument de-pends on Western anthropology for its underpinnings, it distorts and libels the very cultures it is ostensibly defend-ing by implying that individual rights have no place in them. As Jack Donnelly points out in his exhaustive study *Univer-*

sal Human Rights in Theory and Practice, claims by Asian or third-world despotisms and their apologists about indigenous cultures are usually self-serving misrepresentations: "Arguments of cultural relativism are far too often made by economic and political elites that have long since left traditional culture behind. . . . The cynicism of many claims of cultural relativism can also be seen in the fact that far too often they are for foreign consumption only. The same elites that raise culture as a defense against external criticisms based on universal human rights often ruthlessly suppress inconvenient local customs, whether of the majority or of a minority."[8]

Regardless of the disingenuous purposes they sometimes serve, what all these usages have in common is the assumption that gesturing to "culture" explains much about human behavior; that belonging to a certain culture at a certain period in history causes everyone in that culture to believe certain things or to act in certain ways; and furthermore that whatever is described as "cultural"—unless it happens to be part of one's own culture—is in theory (though not always in practice) beyond criticism. But this formulation raises many questions, some of them obvious, others more subtle. A culture can be logically held responsible only for actions that the vast majority of its members commit, or beliefs that they hold. Yet habits and beliefs vary enormously among individuals, not just in a large, modern "culture" but in any culture of which we have detailed historical knowledge. Look at the drastic differences of opinion and conduct among the thinkers in tiny Athens two and a half millennia ago. If you prefer a non-Western example, consider the equally wide disagreements among the philosophers of classical India.

And there are other problems with believing that an entity called culture somehow exists to control human beings as methodically as Mead and Benedict asserted. In this worldview, where does culture come from? Like human beings themselves, it has to be a product of evolution, a complicated form of adaptation that developed over time between a distinct group of people and their particular environment. The differences between cultures—highlighted by the tendency of early anthropologists to generalize on the basis of pre-modern peoples in remote settings—seemed to those anthropologists to imply that human nature is endlessly malleable. Potentially, the number of different modes of physical and spiritual adaptation to an ambiguous world should be without limit.

"The vast proportion of all individuals who are born into any society," claimed Benedict, "always and whatever the idiosyncrasies of its institutions, assume, as we have seen, the behaviour dictated by that society. This fact is always interpreted by the carriers of that culture as being due to the fact that their particular institutions reflect an ultimate and universal sanity." According to this theory, which has been more frequently challenged since the collapse of communism cast doubt on it, most people will do or believe almost anything if their culture demands it. Culture defined in this uncompromising way is an anthropological form of Lamarckism: the inheritance of infinitely varied acquired characteristics. Yet the list of characteristics that all known cultures past or present have in common is quite long.

According to the Yale anthropologist George P. Murdock, writing in 1945, it runs the alphabetical gamut from age-grading, athletic sports, and bodily adornment to visiting, weaving, and weather control, including such important institutions as calendar, division of labor, ethics, folklore, funeral rites, government, inheritance rules, kinship, marriage, medicine, personal names, property rights, religious ritual, sexual restrictions, status differentiation, trade, and much else.[9] Although their forms vary widely, the fundamental arrangements of human social life seem to transcend culture.

The doctrine of omnipotent culture raises not only the question of why different forms of group adaptation evolved as they did, but also in what sense they can all be said to meet the needs of their "carriers." In some cases economic factors are evidently important. The American South before the Civil War, for example, clung to slavery long after the rest of the country had given it up, and the perceived need to defend slavery in a hostile world determined much of antebellum Southern culture. But here the explanatory machine has gone into reverse: instead of culture explaining anything on its own, economics explains culture, as it does in traditional Marxism. Of course there are still some who would argue that culture is always determined by economics, and that today's cross-cultural uniformities—such as the worldwide prevalence of blue jeans, Coca-Cola, and rock music—are simply a matter of dominant American export industries. Even in this example, however, much more is at stake than products. You still have to explain why people buy those products and the attitudes that often accompany them.

Does their culture make them do it? Economic pressure would seem to work the other way; jeans and Big Macs are expensive in most places outside the United States. What cultural or economic motivation would there be for buying them in, say, Peking or Paris? What is gained by using the word "cultural" in any explanation for French or Chinese adoption of certain American tastes and products? Why did the United States achieve such power and importance in the world while the other large, potentially rich nations of the western hemisphere—Brazil, Canada, and Argentina—did not? Why did the ancient Greeks develop drama, democracy, and philosophy while the Hebrews developed Judaism and the Bible? All sorts of historical answers can be hazarded for any of these random questions, but attributing the differences to "culture" is a bit like saying that inches are what make you tall.

Culture is an abstract, collective label for a miscellany of shifting beliefs, practices, and ingenuities of adaptation. It is not an additional entity that controls and explains them. Sometimes it is accurate and useful to point out that certain practices or beliefs are typical within a particular culture. Irresolvable contradictions arise when we go further and assert that a large abstraction, culture, *causes* (or "constructs") beliefs and practices. In discussions of culture or society, the danger of reification—of mistaking a word for a thing and imputing fanciful powers to it—is always great. Far from explaining anything by themselves, the differences between cultures are often the very facts that cry out for explanation.

When pressed, classical anthropologists would sometimes concede that the dominion of culture was not absolute. Some recognition of the possibility of innovation was necessary, not only because innovation had demonstrably occurred, but also because anthropologists themselves were so often writing partly to change social attitudes in their own society. If individuals could never successfully challenge a culture—for example, on its racial attitudes—then Mead and Benedict and other like-minded colleagues were wasting their time. For somewhat the same reason, they found themselves torn between the claim that all moral beliefs are culturally specific and the opposite assertion that the fundamentals of morality are universal. To a non-anthropologist, it would seem that cultural determinism, which holds that all beliefs are the product of culture, contradicts the idea of cultural relativism, which takes the universalistic position that all cultures and the people who inherit them have equal value. In other words, to a cultural determinist, aren't cultural relativists a product of their culture?

No serious proponent of cultural relativism regards it as merely a feature of twentieth-century European thought. Like other forms of relativism, cultural relativism has to make an exception for itself: it must be the one belief that transcends culture and is true without qualification. This exception is a paradoxical form of the acknowledgment that not all individuals are always bound by the standards of their culture. Otherwise how could there be anthropologists? Yet those anthropologists' recognition of individual variation within cultures was often brief and inconspicuous, even grudging. In the last few pages of *Anthropology and Modern Life,* Franz Boas, the mentor of Margaret Mead and Ruth Benedict, announced somewhat defensively:

> It hardly seems necessary to consider culture a mystic entity that exists outside the society of its individual carriers, and that moves by its own force. The life of a society is carried on by individuals who act singly and jointly under the stress of the tradition in which they have grown up and surrounded by the products of their own activities and those of their forbears. These determine the direction of their activities positively or negatively. They may proceed to act and think according to the transmitted patterns or they may be led to move in opposite directions. . . .
>
> The forces that bring about the changes are active in the individuals composing the social groups, not in the abstract culture.[10]

What exactly are the "forces" that bring about what "changes"? Boas is frustratingly unclear about which factors enable some individuals to think or act in ways counter to the prevailing opinions and practices of their culture. (The contemporary anthropologist James L. Watson, of whom we will see more later, seems to echo Boas without solving any of these problems: "Culture is a set of ideas, re-actions, and expectations that is constantly changing as people and groups themselves change."[11]) Allowing much room for unpredictable individual variation, after all, would upset not just the omnipotence of culture but the whole theoretical basis for a scientific anthropology.

Another reason Boas, Mead, and Benedict all laid such emphasis on culture was that, writing in the 1920s and '30s, they saw the alternative as a dangerous biological determin-ism that led directly to eugenics and doctrines of racial infe-riority. With Adolf Hitler on the horizon or clearly in view, all three denounced racial prejudice as a destructive atavism both at home and abroad. In their attacks on racism, the doctrines of cultural determinism and cultural relativism had to be tacitly abandoned as inconsistent with the argumentative needs of the moment: racial prejudices were neither an irresistible product of culture nor beyond criticism. Speaking as scientists, they emphasized that race and culture were totally different concepts, that one race might encompass many cultures and one culture many races. (To be sure, they occasionally forgot themselves and referred to the spread of "white culture" as a misfortune.) Today, much of the obsession among social scientists and humanists with cultural explanations for belief and behav-ior comes from, or at least is related to, the same set of fears: biological explanations for any but the most innocu-ous aspects of human social life lead to racism, eugenics, even genocide. Reflected in the gene pool is the image of Auschwitz.

Despite this inflammatory set of associations, a revived

interest in Darwinism and heritable traits during the 1980s and '90s returned genetic explanations for some kinds and proportion of human behavior to scholarly respectability. The Human Genome Project is one of the major scientific enterprises of our time. Nevertheless, that collective beliefs and behavior depend on the "cultural construction" of reality, and are therefore arbitrary, remains an emotionally defended article of faith in many academic circles, at least in the abstract. Yet that doctrine too suffers from grave problems that have been pointed out many times.

One of its greatest difficulties is that if taken literally, the doctrine of cultural construction denies any objective status to science and scientific medicine. Is the earth really an approximate sphere that orbits the sun, or is that merely one culture's way of conceiving it? It would seem willfully ignorant today to act on any alternative theory, no matter what culture one hails from. Are the creation myths of the Lakota Sioux as accurate a form of explanation for human origins as the theory of evolution? They once served certain social and psychological purposes, and one may hold the people who imagined them in high respect, but nobody today who seriously wants to know where we came from would grant such myths the same status as modern evolutionary biology. One is culture, the other science: not the same thing. After Stalin for ideological reasons ordered the scientists under his control to follow the theories of Trofim Lysenko about the inheritance of acquired characteristics, Soviet biology became a laughingstock, not because it was not Western or bourgeois but because scientifically it was nonsense.

Medicine exhibits the conflicts between science and culture at their most dramatic. Is epilepsy caused by a malfunction in the biochemistry of the brain or, as the Hmong tribes of Laos (a people who in their homeland suffered a 50 percent infant mortality rate) believe, by a spirit that can be exorcised? Anne Fadiman's fascinating 1997 book *The Spirit Catches You and You Fall Down* narrates at length the conflict between American doctors and a Hmong family in California over the treatment of their epileptic infant daughter, Lia. The basic issue was hard to evade: "Each had accurately noted the same symptoms, but Dan [the attending doctor] would have been surprised to hear that they were caused by soul loss, and Lia's parents would have been surprised to hear that they were caused by an electrochemical storm inside their daughter's head that had been stirred up by the misfiring of aberrant brain cells."[12] How far will cultural relativism get us here? Not far enough, if saving the life and health of the child is the goal.

With great sensitivity and even admiration for the Hmong family's traditional beliefs, Fadiman's book documents excruciatingly the price the family paid—severe, permanent brain damage to their afflicted child—for clinging to the healing practices of their medically uninformed culture. The ambivalent author feels so drawn to the family and the plight it faces in a strange land that she pleads, "I don't think it would be too much to ask them [Western doctors] to *acknowledge* their patients' realities. . . ." But, as she also points out, Lia's doctors had in fact made a major effort to understand the Hmong culture of the parents. Humane acknowledgment of the helpless stranger as a human being equal to oneself is not the same thing as granting the stranger's medical views equal status. On that issue, by the end of the story, the conclusion of the book is inevitably one-sided, however diffident the author feels about saying so. Late in the book she recounts an occasion when

> I started to lament the insensitivity of Western medicine. The epidemiologist looked at me sharply. "*Western medicine saves lives*," she said. Oh. Right. I had to keep reminding myself of that. It was all that cold, linear, Cartesian, non-Hmong-like thinking which saved my father from colon cancer, saved my husband and me from infertility, and, if she had swallowed her anticonvulsants from the start, might have saved Lia from brain damage.[13]

Because of episodes like this, how to "manage" cultural diversity has become a major issue in medicine and medical education. A recent textbook for nursing schools declares, in more stilted words than Fadiman's, that "The promotion of diversity moves beyond tolerance, patronization, generosity, and 'good deeds,' and even beyond common decency, to confronting differences and developing the flexibility that allows appreciation and respect for both differences and similarities." Multicultural practices are necessary in medicine, the authors argue, because "we are a diverse people and becoming increasingly so in this country." After enthusiastically endorsing cultural relativism, however, they find it necessary to warn that relativism "has its limitations. A naive, blanket acceptance of beliefs and practices as functionally or ethically neutral may be harmful and may lead providers to be inappropriately inactive."[14] Culture is culture, in other words, but medicine is medicine. In the last analysis, how many Western multiculturalists would risk their own lives or those of their children on the theory that Western medicine is merely a product of Western culture, neither better nor worse than that of any other people?

Practitioners of the discipline called cultural studies have tried, in a variety of provocative ways, to challenge the status of modern medicine and the physical sciences as fundamentally rhetorical disciplines that thoroughly reflect European values, are male-oriented and logocentric. Yet it is hard to believe that these challenges are meant to be taken at face value, except perhaps as a complaint from humanists that their own disciplines are undervalued in a world where science is considered the only form of reliable knowledge. And the same old problem of relativism surfaces here in a slightly different guise: what is the status of the claim that even the most empirically tested conclusions of science are culturally constructed? Is it really true, or just one more cultural construction?[15] We seem to have reached what philosophers call the Cretan-liar paradox, in which we are at a loss either to believe or to disbelieve a Cretan who tells us that all members of his nation are chronic liars.

If the belief in the cultural construction of reality is itself a cultural construction, what in "Western culture" today causes so many Western intellectuals to believe it? Why do they so often inconsistently combine a belief in cultural constructivism and relativism with moral indignation toward the practices and attitudes (racial, sexual, political) of their own society? Commenting on the intellectual phenomenon of "moral nihilism charged with moral fury," the philosopher Michael Polanyi declared in 1965: "This paradoxical combination is new in history and deserves a new name; I have called it *moral inversion.*"[16]

Regardless of theoretical positions and their ultimate foundations, the claim that every "culture" and all of its expressions should be equally respected is too sentimental for anyone to follow consistently, though it gets a lot of play in the abstract. Even Kroeber felt that his anthropological colleagues paid too little attention to the possibility of "fixed, pan-human, if not absolute, values."[17] What cultural relativism now usually amounts to in practice is that only those aspects of non-European cultures that seem compatible with Western feminism and at least a minimal notion of human rights are held up as examples of diversity. Few American multiculturalists are enthusiastic about the treatment of women in Saudi Arabia (the fact that they are forbidden to drive cars led to outrage in the media during the Gulf War) or, worse yet, Afghanistan under the Taliban; female circumcision in parts of Africa has lately illuminated another boundary of cultural relativism in the West. The mere fact that an Asian or African culture has practiced a custom since time immemorial is not always sufficient to legitimize it. Even the most sympathetic Western enthusiasts occasionally practice the moral universalism they profess to have seen through in theory.

As in the United States, organized feminists in other countries, though favorable in theory to multiculturalism, frequently protest against traditional cultural demands on women and uphold individual freedom—for example, the opportunity for women to receive education on the same basis as men, to express their opinions without fear of retaliation, to practice professions, to bear as many or as few children as they wish. Such a universalist, even post-cultural position was taken by many speakers at the 1995 United Nations Conference on Women, held in China, who were surprisingly critical of practices in (often their own) poor non-white countries. Because not all practices from alien cultures pass muster even with the professionally tolerant, the multiculturalism festivals held in many American college towns are sometimes reduced, like movie travelogues of the 1940s, to celebrating little more than the traditional foods and costumes that third world peoples haul out on special occasions. Meanwhile the "cultural diversity" practiced in university hiring and admissions has almost nothing to do with culture but offers a justification, in academically familiar language, for affirmative-action categories that are really based on physical characteristics or ancestry.

One conclusion these contradictory and often figurative uses of *culture* suggest is that the entities the word used to identify, which were always more fluid and slippery than many anthropologists liked to admit, are now close to moribund. Like angels, cultures in the abstract inspire sentimental regard today partly because so few Americans have ever met one. Not that there are *no* observable differences in America today among ethnic groups, regions, religious groups, or social classes. But with rare exceptions the differences are too slight and transient to speak of "cultures" without watering the term down to the point where it ceases to denote anything in particular. At the start of the twenty-first century, the residues of cultures in the strong sense defined by early twentieth-century anthropologists are rapidly losing throughout most of the developed world—in the United States have almost entirely lost— their hold over their imputed members. The real differences among people are less and less attributable to cultures of origin. A culture capable of dictating its members' thoughts and behavior to the extent that Ruth Benedict thought normal could do so only by keeping them isolated from countervailing influences. Cultures as isolated as that, however, have been growing rarer for centuries. When real cultural conflict erupts today, in Rwanda or Indonesia or the former Yugoslavia, the spectacle is so atavistic and unexpected that the rest of the world is reduced to impotent horror—at best trying tardily, as in Kosovo, to put broken pieces back together.

The doctrines of cultural relativism and determinism derived from anthropologists' study of tiny, exceptional groups, most of them living on islands in the farther reaches of the Pacific, on Indian reservations in western North America, or in remote parts of Africa. Those cultures were fast losing their distinctness even as they were being studied. Their isolation from other groups and their primitiveness were explicit reasons for studying them, since (as Ruth Benedict explained) they presented in simplified terms "a laboratory in which we may study the diversity of the human institutions."[18] Modern civilization by contrast was too complicated and mixed for satisfactory analysis. The steamship, the telegraph, and the newspaper had already gone a long way toward breaking down cultural separation in most of the world, fifty years before the jet plane and nearly a century before the Internet.

Although Benedict, like Boas and other anthropologists before and since her time, wrote her best-selling book to persuade her readers of the equality and relativity of cultures, she had to admit in passing that modern America was nothing like the backward, homogeneous tribes to which she devoted most of her pages:

> Modern civilization has grown too complex for adequate analysis except as it is broken up for the purpose into small artificial sections. And these partial analyses are inadequate because so many outside factors cannot be controlled. A survey of any one group involves individuals out of opposed heterogeneous groups, with different standards, social aims, home relations, and morality. The interrelation of these groups is too complicated to evaluate in the necessary detail. In primitive society, the cultural tradition is simple enough to be contained within the knowledge of individual adults, and the manners and morals of the group are moulded to one well-defined general pattern. It is possible to estimate the interrelation of traits in this simple environment in a way which is impossible in the cross-currents of our complex civilization.[19]

Even by the early 1930s modern civilization was so different from the fading entities on which anthropologists based their whole concept of culture that anatomizing the United States or Europe in terms of that concept was impossible.

Given Benedict's purposes and outlook, this plaintive passage is an extraordinary admission. Even among the American Indian and New Guinea tribes on which she lavished so much attention, the first stages of post-culturalism, in which technology begins the long process of displacing custom, were clearly visible. Two-thirds of a century later, that kind of primitive culture has reached its vanishing point nearly everywhere, yet the terminology and assumptions to which the study of it gave rise are more ingrained than ever. The example of the Zulu neatly encapsulates both of these facts at the same time. Their spears can be described as "cultural weapons" precisely because they represent quaint survivals from a vanished way of life. If they could be used effectively as weapons in modern warfare, nobody would call them cultural. Yet they symbolize a culture, which makes their preservation seem a duty to their possessors and an admirable form of solidarity to Western aficionados of otherness, who would be disappointed if the Zulus gave them up.

In his book about Everest expeditions, John Krakauer reports on another once-isolated traditional culture that now shows signs of breaking up, breaking down, assimilating, becoming Westernized, modernized, Americanized, globalized, hybridized—all these terms and more are available for such cases. The Himalayan Sherpas now wear blue jeans and Chicago Bulls T-shirts; they often spend their evenings watching videos of Arnold Schwarzenegger movies. Some visitors feel let down. Krakauer does not agree. "It seems more than a little patronizing," he writes, "for Westerners to lament the loss of the good old days when life in the Khumbu was so much simpler and more picturesque. Most of the people who live in this rugged country seem to have no desire to be severed from the modern world or the untidy flow of human progress. The last thing the Sherpas want is to be preserved as specimens in an anthropological museum."[20]

In contrast to the now-fading traditional life of the Sherpas and the Zulus, the "culture" of the Internet has none of the characteristics of a real culture. It is not a total way of life; it did not evolve among a distinct people; nobody inherited it or was raised in it; it makes no moral demands, has no religion at its center, and produces no art. Although complex, its rules are purely procedural. The same is true, in slightly different ways, of the "culture" of the CIA, the press, or General Motors. Nobody doubts that within contemporary American society, differences of perception and behavior exist that bear some relation to divisions of race, class, sex, occupation, and a myriad of other group distinctions. But with rare exceptions the connections are too approximate, the differences too small, the areas of overlap too large, the pace of change too fast, to make the notion of culture anything but a source of confusion. The word has come to be used so loosely because those who use it have no organic relationship to a real inherited culture and no clear conception of what such a relationship would be like.

Apart from WASPs and the children of immigrants, few Americans grow up knowing the ancestral language through which an ancestral culture would be transmitted. Generations of intermarriage have given most Americans multiple ancestral languages. According to the 1990 census, 86 percent of all American residents over the age of five spoke no language at home other than English. Notwithstanding incessant talk about cultural diversity and the need to educate students for a global economy, fewer and fewer universities require the study of a foreign language for admission or graduation, something that was nearly universal in the supposedly more ethnocentric 1950s.

Except on the most superficial level, few Americans inherit traditions distinct from those of different ethnic backgrounds. One result is what Freud aptly called "the narcissism of minor differences," adding that "it is a convenient and relatively harmless satisfaction of the inclination to aggression, by means of which cohesion between the members of the community is made easier."[21] Many black Americans exaggerate and sentimentalize their connections to a lost cultural homeland—Kwanzaa was invented in Los Angeles during the 1960s—but many Italian and Irish Americans do exactly the same. So do American-born Hispanics who speak of rediscovering their heritage through watching Univision, the Los Angeles–based Spanish-language cable network. In an era when identity is more elusive and changeable than ever before, everyone at a given level of affluence has access to the assortment of myths and products that now help define it from moment to moment.

Can the same person belong to several cultures at the

same time? Presumably yes if a race, an ethnic group, a class, a sex, a region, an employer could all have their own "cultures." But then the whole concept loses even more of its shape. (We are not talking yet about border situations or intermarriage, but about unambiguously belonging.) For simultaneous membership in more than one culture to be meaningful, you would have to conceive of each individual as a marionette whose strings are held by multiple hands. The result would be paralysis, or a puppet's equivalent of schizophrenia.

With its tight, narrow definitions of influence and belonging, the classical anthropological concept of culture never applied comfortably to big, modern societies. When squeezed, it always bulged with insoluble conundrums. As time passed it explained less and less about the country whose social scientists had popularized it so successfully. There was too much individual and group variation within the same society to speak meaningfully of a single American culture, and as the country matured, the determinants of variation were less and less attributable to separate ancestral cultures. Later anthropologists' efforts to restate or modify the concept have little relevance for our purposes; their impact was felt mostly within the discipline itself. Hence by the end of the twentieth century, *culture* in American usage had a strong set of connotations but no precise meaning.

Chapter Two

Multiculturalism
as Museum

Recently a student in my twentieth-century poetry class came to see me for advice on how to improve her grade, which at that point was an A–. As is so often the case, her real problem turned out to be quite different from the ostensible one.

She is the youngest person in her family, its first member to be born in the United States and the only one with an English first name. Her parents and three older siblings had come from Korea a few years before her birth, first to New York, then to Philadelphia. When she started public school, by state law she was placed in a bilingual program, though her parents had deliberately seen to it that she already spoke English far better than Korean. As a result, much of her early education was a waste of time. "I spent fifth grade brushing up on my poker," she told me, and in fact she began to gamble at a precocious age.

Because she still speaks little Korean and her parents' English is limited, the difficulties of intergenerational communication are extreme. Nevertheless she felt the same pressures that so many Asian-American children feel to excel in school, to attend an Ivy League university, and to become a doctor or lawyer or, like her father, an engineer. Her parents hired tutors and arranged for more educational enrichment than she could bear. Alas, unlike the stereotypical Asian-American student, she was backward at math. On the other hand, her English is far more articulate and subtle than that of most North American university students.

She began college as a psychology major, then changed to anthropology. Recently she switched again to English; her ambition, she said, had always been to become a professor of English. Penn State is not an urban university, and she felt isolated in several senses—not only because there were few other Asian-American students in her field, but because few other Penn State undergraduates had ever felt anything like the same degree of family pressure to achieve. Although different members of her family professed Christianity, Buddhism, and militant atheism, the only time she felt she had an understanding peer group was when she attended a suburban high school with Jewish classmates who suffered from parents with similarly high expectations. These pressures to some degree estranged her from her large extended family; at the age of nineteen she was self-supporting. For two years she had been working her way through college as a chef in an Italian restaurant.

Does her eccentric path make her a candidate for therapy? Not, I think, of any traditional kind. The anomalies of identity that trouble her have little to do with the conventional categories of psychopathology. Nor does the identity politics that flourishes in most American universities have anything to offer her. The kind of multiculturalism that put her in ostensibly bilingual classrooms as a child would be utterly beside the point; this young woman describes herself as "American to the core," though the core is unstable and certainly contains elements her parents brought with them from Asia.

She can be called bicultural only in a very limited sense. Emphasizing her differences from other Americans would simply intensify what she perceives as her difficulties—difficulties that are a strange but increasingly familiar mixture of ordinary late twentieth-century post-adolescent adjustment with the ambiguities of ethnic assimilation to an American way of life that is itself ambiguous. Her experiences have alienated her not only from her family but from her classmates, whose own families' experience of immigration took place several or many generations ago. The norms of Korean culture have ceased to bind her, if they ever did, but no equally authoritative set of norms has taken their place. Instead of the familiar story of assimilation, which substitutes the demands and choices of one culture for another, she has grown up in a historically unprecedented environment where the concept of "culture," though constantly invoked, has ceased to have much meaning.

Her situation is a dramatic example of post-cultural-ism. Consider, first, the issue of language. The bilingual programs she was forced to endure exist today not so much to ease the transition of non-English-speaking students into an English-speaking educational environment—their official justification when the federal Bilingual Education Act was passed in 1968—but rather to preserve minority "cultures" by ensuring that the children of immigrants continue to speak their parents' languages (of which Spanish is by far the most common). The true roots of bilingual education lay in the ethnic politics of the Southwest, and most studies suggest that it fails to help students make the transition to English. According to the *New York Times* of January 31, 1999, although other language groups do better, 90 percent of the Spanish-speaking students in New York City are still not ready for mainstream classes after three years.

The disadvantages of such a policy to students who after all will live their lives in an English-speaking environment have become increasingly evident. Thus overwhelming numbers of immigrant parents have turned against bilingualism in schools. Parents in several states have filed suit to get their kids out of bilingual classes, and a 1998 poll taken by the nonpartisan group Public Agenda found, according to the same *New York Times Magazine* article, that 75 percent of recent immigrants (including 56 percent of recent Hispanic immigrants) opposed bilingual education. In a June 1998 referendum the voters of California by a wide margin virtually abolished bilingual education in their state. This result could not have come about had many natural-ized citizens not rejected linguistic preservationism in favor of having the schools teach their children English as rapidly as possible.

Of course, most multiculturalists would describe such a defeat as a depressing victory for monoculturalism rather than post-culturalism. That is, the immigrant parents could merely be trading one culture for another on mercenary grounds. Certainly they were willing to abandon their ancestral language, at least as a first language for their children. But we are not dealing here with self-hatred or xenophobia. Most immigrants and non-immigrants alike believe that retaining or learning a second language is a good thing—but only if children learn to speak English as their primary tongue.

The right of individuals to speak Spanish or Korean in private or even public contexts is not the same thing as the "right" of a group to have the public schools teach its children in Spanish. One could argue with equal plausibility that children have a right to be taught in English, even if their parents' wishes are otherwise. Encouragingly, even in households where Spanish is spoken, 74 percent of all persons over the age of five speak English "very well" or "well," according to the 1990 census. But while language is the most important medium through which a culture transmits its demands, learning English in the United States does not make one part of a "culture" in the same sense that a Mexican artisan or Korean engineer belonged to such an entity before emigrating.

Discussions of multiculturalism in America usually emphasize the growing number of Americans of Hispanic or Asian descent. A century after the height of immigration, the United States continues to receive far more immigrants than any other country in the world. In 1998 the Census Bureau reported with some fanfare that 9.6 percent of U.S. residents had been born elsewhere, the most since 1930 though far below the peak reached in the 1910 census. About half of all foreign-born residents came from Latin America or the Caribbean; a quarter were from Asia. (Racially speaking, the Census Bureau identified 68 percent of all foreign-born residents and 65 percent of those who arrived in the 1990s as white, though for reasons we shall see in the next chapter the Census Bureau's racial categories are at best debatable.)[1] But with an exogamy rate of over 40 percent for people aged under thirty-five of Hispanic descent and 50 percent for people of Asian descent born in the United States, those two hugely varied census categories continue to project identities distinct from the rest of the population only *because* their numbers are constantly replenished by new immigration.[2] As new immigrants appear, the children of the preceding generation merge rapidly into the larger scene.

Again, consider my intrepid student's prospects. What kind of profession will she end up in after she completes her degree and leaves the Italian restaurant? Whom will she marry, if she marries at all? What religion, if any, will she practice? How will she raise her children, assuming she has children? Korean culture, Mexican culture, any traditional culture would once have prescribed a limited range of answers to these questions, answers that she might have found either reassuring or confining, depending on her own temperament. In the United States at the end of the twentieth century, the concept of culture offered no answers to any of them. The woman is on her own, part of a populace as free as any has ever been to make her own decisions. No wonder if she, like so many people, occasionally becomes nostalgic for a world that offered a more secure identity and required less individual initiative.

Learning Korean or masquerading in ancestral dress would not help. "Under modern conditions," says Benjamin Barber in A Place for Us,

> where the environment for natural community has been undermined by secularism, by utilitarianism, and by the erosion of "natural" social ties, many communities claiming traditional or natural identities must make strenuously artificial efforts to reconstitute themselves as the organic natural communities they no longer are or can be. . . . American-born Polish- and African-Americans may identify with remembered or reinvented cultural roots, but they quickly discern, when they visit their ethnic homelands, how remote those hypothetical identities are from the largely deracinated Americans they have inevitably become.[3]

A good example is another young woman I know from Detroit who has suddenly discovered her French-Canadian heritage and wishes eagerly to learn more about it. She speaks no French, however, and sees no point in learning any. Her French Canadianism is a purely contemporary, post-cultural construct—what one sociologist calls a "symbolic ethnicity" that can be worn or not according to mood or circumstance—designed to make her feel less naked around black or Puerto Rican students who aggressively assert their own identities.[4]

Contrasting this metaphorical French Canadianism with the real thing demonstrates the life-or-death importance of language to cultures that are determined to survive against the odds. The Canadian philosopher Charles Taylor, who has devoted much of his attention recently to multicultural issues in his own country, describes some policies that successive Quebec governments have instituted to this end:

> For instance, Quebec has passed a number of laws in the field of language. One regulates who can send their children to English-language schools (not francophones or immigrants); another requires that businesses with more than fifty employees be run in French; a third outlaws commercial signage in any language other than French. In other words, restrictions have been placed on Quebeckers by their government, in the name of their collective goal of survival, which in other Canadian communities might easily be disallowed by virtue of the Charter [the Canadian equivalent of the Bill of Rights].[5]

The premise of such legislation, much more draconian than American laws mandating bilingualism, is obvious: that without these protections the French language and the culture it embodies would continue to die out as French-speaking Canadians joined the more numerous and prosperous Anglophone civilization on both sides of the forty-ninth parallel. Cultural harmony and acceptance of linguistic diversity are seen as a recipe for assimilation; to survive even in its stronghold, French requires exclusivity enforced by law.

Whatever one thinks of the Quebec government's policies, its analysis of the future is probably correct. Even these laws to safeguard their language are not enough for many French Canadians, who seek nothing less than an independent state. When a referendum on Quebec sovereignty narrowly lost in October 1995, the province's premier blamed the result on outside money and the "ethnic vote"— a notorious expression of the xenophobia that is probably inseparable from any vigorous effort to preserve much more of a culture than its food and folktales. Another referendum will probably be held when the independence movement thinks it has a good chance of winning.

For all but a tiny proportion of the North American population—Vietnamese or Cuban immigrant families in certain enclaves, religious minorities such as the Old Order Amish or the Lubavitchers, French Canadians in rural districts of Quebec—the connection with an ancestral culture is now so vestigial that whether to assert or ignore it has become entirely a matter of choice. Taco salad, pizza, stir fry, or the globe-trotting Big Mac? Take your pick. The expanding reach of a homogenizing federal government, universal access to the same products and television programs, interstate highways, and a restlessly mobile population have drastically reduced regional differences as well as ethnic ones in the past half-century. As ethnic studies programs began to do in the seventies and eighties, regional studies programs now dot the academic world like grave markers after a plague. The University of Colorado has a Center of the American West, which competes with the University of Nebraska's Center for Great Plains Studies, the Center for the Study of the Southwest at Southwest Texas State University, and the University of Arizona's Southwest Center. Radford University in southwestern Virginia and nearby East Tennessee State University share the study of Appalachia.

The South, which until the civil rights legislation of the 1960s was the most profoundly different American region, now sports a rapidly increasing number of centers and institutes for the study of its culture, a sure sign of its decline. No more singing "Dixie" and waving the Confederate flag at football games, practices that many colleges have banned. Most of Stephen Foster is gone forever. Wal-Mart, the Xanadu of rootless consumerism, has its headquarters in Bentonville, Arkansas.

Sometimes progress takes the form of amnesia. In the late 1970s I reminded a class of Virginia undergraduates that when their parents were their age, the university had been racially segregated by state law. Most of them didn't believe me; the idea was just too far-fetched. A typical Virginian of fifty or a hundred years ago would not recognize his native state, whose social and racial attitudes (not to mention suburban sprawl) now approximate those of the rest of the country.

In the past decade regional encyclopedias have become a booming product for publishers, most often focusing either on places like the South and New York City, which attract a lot of newcomers who want to bone up on the vanishing local lore, or on the mythical Old West. It is all very picturesque and antiquarian, at best an attempt to memorialize a mixture of good and bad traditions that have lost their force, at worst another form of self-deception about identity. Tombstone, home of the O.K. Corral, survives as a tourist trap filled with movie fans from Germany, while the most popular bar and grill in Prescott, another Arizona Wild West town, offers Cajun beef Stroganoff. Amid its endless strip malls, Richmond, Virginia, the capital of the Confederacy in the 1860s and of massive resistance to integration a century later, now boasts a combination Irish pub and bagel shop called O'Brienstein's, which (like many other enterprises around the country) sells objects that no traditionalist would recognize as bagels. In New York City the venerable Pastrami King delicatessen recently added chicken curry and beef lo mein to its menu.

The universal familiarity of all these dishes indicates not that many cultures flourish here but that innocuous morsels of each are now part of something else, something often miscalled American culture—dynamic, inclusive, a now truly national melting pot despite the recent unpopularity of the term. In fact, what we have is no longer a culture at all in the traditional sense of the word. If it were, it would exclude more and at the same time take more for granted, as it did before 1914 in the heyday of immigration. In a living culture E. D. Hirsch would not write a book called *Cultural Literacy* to teach native-born Americans things they would already know if they were part of one.

In the United States, multiculturalism is not only the policy of the federal government, the mainstream press, Hollywood, and education at all levels; some forms of it also have considerable support from the general public. For such a recently coined term, however, the lack of any generally accepted meaning is surprising. Terence Turner, a skeptical University of Chicago anthropologist, took a stab at a definition in 1992: "As a code word for minority demands for separate recognition in academic and other cultural institutions, multiculturalism tends to become a form of identity politics in which the concept of culture becomes merged with that of ethnic identity."[6] Like most people who write about it, Turner seemed unaware that the word first arose not as an academic or scholarly term but within the context of Canadian politics.

According to Lexis-Nexis, its first American appearance was in a *New York Times* report of a 1971 speech by Canadian Prime Minister Pierre Trudeau. During the 1960s, as part of the soul-searching that accompanied Canada's centennial as a nation, the federal government established a Commission on Bilingualism and Biculturalism. Its purpose was to mollify French Canadians who felt like second-class citizens, and simultaneously to strengthen the country's unity by giving the French language and French-Canadian culture equal status with English. As we have seen, this effort was at best debatably successful. But one consequence, at least, was predictable: other ethnic groups who felt neglected demanded that their languages and cultures, whether native to Canada or imported by immigrants, receive the same exalted status as English and French. Anything less was discrimination. The commission's preliminary report in 1965, according to the *Oxford English Dictionary,* launched *multiculturalism* as a synonym for "the Canadian mosaic."

What North American government could resist that kind of pressure? In October 1971 Trudeau announced to the Ukrainian Congress in Winnipeg, Manitoba, what he called a "multiculturalism" plan (the October 10 *Times* put the unfamiliar word in quotation marks) to help other ethnic groups besides French- and English-descended Canadians preserve and develop their cultures. Within a few years the government of Canada had a minister for multiculturalism. By the mid-1980s the word was becoming commonplace south of the forty-ninth parallel. The rest is history of several kinds in many countries, for not since the telephone has a Canadian invention been so widely and rapidly adopted. Probably the most notable victory for multiculturalism in its country of origin was the creation in early 1999 of a self-governing territory for the Inuit (Eskimos) called Nunavut, where an Arctic population of 27,000 occupies one-fifth of the entire area of Canada and has three official languages.

Canadians often assert proudly that their humane nation has preserved more of its native and immigrant cultures than the United States has. The creation of Nunavut is only the most dramatic example. Just as Quebec has laws to protect its language and culture against those of English Canada, so the federal government has created a host of

regulations since the 1960s to defend English-Canadian culture against influences from the United States. During the
same period, life in all parts of Canada has been moving
steadily closer to the American norm of free individual
choice among a host of once-exclusive alternatives. Even
Nunavut's brand-new capital has its own Kentucky Fried
Chicken outlet. While a sympathetic non-Canadian who
once lived in Canada feels reluctant to make predictions, it
should be instructive to see how much real cultural distinctiveness will survive among which groups, who depend on
what degree of government support, and for how long.

As anyone who has inspected the burgeoning literature
about it knows, multiculturalism—whether in Canada, the
United States, or other places—often means the militant,
even separatist assertion of non-European-derived identities against a supposedly oppressive European-American
dominant culture. Peter McLaren, a professor of education
at UCLA, distinguishes four varieties of multiculturalism,
the first three of which he rejects as insufficiently liberating
for beleaguered minorities: "conservative multiculturalism,"
"liberal multiculturalism," and "left-liberal multiculturalism." In opposition to what McLaren calls "white terror," he
endorses "critical and resistance multiculturalism," which
rejects the "oppressively universalistic humanism" of liberalism and demands social revolution. An easygoing pluralism within an evolving national framework is not for him.
"Critical multiculturalism," he explains, "interrogates the
construction of difference and identity in relation to a radical politics. It is positioned against the neo-imperial ro-
mance with monoglot ethnicity grounded in a shared or

'common' experience of 'America' that is associated with conservative and liberal strands of multiculturalism."[7]

Whatever else this doctrine means, its hostility toward the United States as historically constituted, as well as toward the cultural inheritance of Europe, is obvious. This radical version, sometimes called "difference multiculturalism," can now be found in many educational institutions and frequently gives rise to extreme curricular effects. The concept of culture being so nebulous, race often takes its place without acknowledgment. On March 11, 1998, a few months before California held its referendum on bilingual education, the *New York Times* published a story with the following lead: "To increase the cultural diversity of the curriculum, the San Francisco school board is considering a plan to require that at least half the books assigned to every high school student in the district be by authors of color."

Notice that nothing is said about what colors these authors must be, let alone what their books should be like. For this school board white is white, color is color, and both are cultures. "Our culture," said Dr. Dan Kelly, vice president of the board, "is no longer Anglo-Saxon, Teutonic, Celtic. In San Francisco, the public school population is only thirteen percent what you'd call white." (That is, what you'd call white if you counted all Hispanic students as non-white.) The school board mentioned no actual authors, let alone book titles; that would be beside the point. Any non-white authors will serve the purpose better than any white ones. Culture is color. It would be hard to find a better example of confusion wielding the language of anthropology.

Other examples of "difference" multiculturalism affect

the legal system. In recent American jurisprudence the "cultural defense," as theorized by some lawyers, holds that immigrants from countries with different customs should not be held to a universal legal standard. In a notable example of this defense, a Chinese immigrant who bludgeoned his unfaithful wife to death with a claw hammer was sentenced to probation in New York in 1989, after an anthropologist testified on Chinese men's feelings about adultery. The outcome of this trial might be fairly described as multiculturalism with a vengeance, but less sensational cases raise some of the same problems of cultural relativity versus equal justice. Most cultures recognize that the course of true love has a hard enough time running smoothly under the best of circumstances. Its problems increase by orders of magnitude when another culture gets into the act. In a 1997 case, two Iraqi Shi'ite refugees in Nebraska were charged with sexual assault and statutory rape as a result of their arranged marriages with a pair of underage sisters; the girls' parents were charged with child abuse and contributing to the delinquency of a minor. The defense, predictably, was that the parents and the grooms were simply following the age-old traditions of their own culture.

In both these instances, and many others like them, the most vocal opponents of multicultural relativism were feminists, who as a rule vigorously defend that theory in contexts where women's rights are not threatened. The protection of relatively defenseless individuals, one of the most widely accepted principles of American law, sometimes conflicts with cultural relativism in ways that nobody can ig-

nore. For the point is sometimes made that American attitudes toward the equality of women are not shared by many
of the world's non-European cultures, and that requiring
immigrants to accept them may be no more than another
form of ethnocentrism. "That's just a fact," said the lawyer
for the grooms in the Nebraska case. "And it puts the American liberal in a classic quandary. On the one hand, he
doesn't want to impose his views on other people—he's big
on that—and, on the other hand, he really does."[8]

Whatever one thinks about this conflict of values,
within a generation or two the familiar processes of assimilation are likely to ease the problems caused by Shi'ite or
Chinese marriage customs. But what about American Indians who make concerted efforts to revive their own traditions, claiming with justification that they were here first?*
The last "wild" Indian in the United States literally spent
the last few years of his life in the University of California's
anthropology museum. Although he learned to speak English and made friends among the scholars who studied him,
he never told anyone his real name and died there of tuber-
culosis in 1916, the last survivor of the Yahi people.[9] This
sad, bizarre story symbolizes a fate that many Indian tribes
today are trying hard to avoid. Some of the compromises
they feel obliged to make between ancient heritages and the

---

*I should emphasize here that I mean no disrespect by avoiding the mul-
ticulturalists' term "Native American." Its inaccuracy in implying that the
ancestors of present-day American Indians originated in this hemisphere,
together with its invidious implication that everyone else who lives here
is a foreigner, seems to me reason enough to prefer the traditional term,
which the Census Bureau, most anthropologists, and most Indians still
employ.

needs of the present, however, are deeply unsettling to perceptive multiculturalists.

According to a June 15, 1997, article in *Parade,* a town in Oregon is trying to get the Nez Percé Indians to return to their ancestral valley and simultaneously generate some tourist dollars by building a cultural center that is "culturally correct." As a local high school teacher put it, "We want to create a place where the Nez Percé can come back and be comfortable, a place for them to store and preserve their culture, a place where they can tell their story—and we're doing it because we think it's right." The combination of moral self-congratulation here with confusion about what a culture is (something to store and preserve in a cultural center?) tells a lot about what is really at stake.

Cultural centers in Indian country seem to have many of the same problems as those in cities with no Indian population—once they have been built, people have trouble deciding what they were really for, who should pay the light bills, and whether the project was worth the trouble. In 1993, when I tried to visit the brand-new cultural center and museum on an Apache reservation in Arizona, I found it had already closed for good. Workmen were in the process of transforming it into a casino. Casino gambling on Indian reservations, legitimized by court decisions in the early and mid-nineties, has not only become a (often the) major source of income for the tribes concerned. It has even led to the reconstitution of long-moribund tribal organizations, such as the Pequots of Connecticut, who own one of the largest casinos in the country.

How many believers in equality would begrudge reservation Indians, who have suffered the ills of poverty for so long, an opportunity to make some money, even if it involves an especially crass form of entrepreneurship? But in the wake of this compromise with traditional culture—perhaps as a compensation for it—have come reassertions of identity that raise most of the same questions as other ethnic groups' attempts to keep their home fires from going out. On many reservations, gambling money finances "powwows," a combination of religious event, tourist attraction, and opportunity to revive cultural expressions that have died out. "We have to revive this culture," a Mohegan salesman at Home Depot points out. "So we have a powwow and pass it on and hope the kids will pass it on as well." "The powwows have provided at least a beginning to educate people about the culture," says a Micmac Indian in New Hampshire, once again to an enthralled *New York Times* (August 24, 1997)—"and the ones who need the education most are Native Americans."

A major difficulty with revitalizing Indian identity is that a tiny population is divided among a great many tribes, some of which, in the East and Midwest, retain only the most notional existence. According to the 1990 census there were 1,878,285 American Indians in the United States, which worked out to eight-tenths of 1 percent of the population. Furthermore, like other ethnic or racial categories in the census, "American Indian" is a matter of self-identification, and even where tribes have official definitions of membership they often require only fractional descent. As for the multitude of separate languages that Indians spoke when the Europeans first arrived, the great majority of them are now extinct.

Interestingly enough, the 1990 Indian population had grown by 37.7 percent since the 1980 census, almost four times the rate of increase of the white population. Given that American Indians increase negligibly through immigration, these figures suggest that many people of mixed origins who used to consider themselves white have more recently decided to call themselves Indian. The historian David Hollinger attributes this demographic self-transformation "to the promise of entitlements and to the cultural reality of more positive public attitudes toward Indians."[10] The ambivalent or changing attitudes of these quasi-Indians themselves may be another reason both for the dilution of Indian cultural identity and for current attempts to reassert it.

Things are not much different in those parts of the West where the tribes that were most successful in maintaining their own territories and that mixed least with other ethnic groups are also trying to combat a loss of continuity with their past. On the immense Navajo reservation that straddles Arizona, Colorado, New Mexico, and Utah, young people have been taking up jogging under a grant from Nike. Dressed in their running clothes and shoes, the Navajos in question, handsomely pictured in the August 2, 1998, *New York Times*, look indistinguishable from other joggers, though their running takes them through a more spectacular environment than most. But the program, called Wings of America, is being sold in the language of multiculturalism as a reassertion of Navajo identity. "Running has its roots in the spiritual tradition," says William E. Channing, the president of Wings. "Running increases pride, self-esteem, cultural identity." One of the Navajo running instructors sports a tattoo that proclaims his tribal affiliation. "When I go out, I want people to know I am Navajo," he announced. "It drives me to run harder." In this benign, inoffensive, and even health-giving instance, assimilation has been disguised as its opposite.

Not all expressions of Indian identity are so uncontroversial. What happens when a tribe that has not hunted whales within the memory of anyone now living insists on its rights to resume the practice, this time using a fifty-caliber anti-tank gun with an infrared sight? In 1996 the Makah Nation, numbering some two thousand members on the coast of Washington, applied to the International Whaling Commission, with the support of the Clinton administration, for the right to kill up to five California gray whales a year over five years for ceremonial purposes. The tribe cited an 1855 treaty, and an exemption from the worldwide whaling ban was duly granted in October 1997. Because they had last pursued whales in the 1920s and were understandably rusty with the harpoon, the Makah decided to use weapons that would save them from the humiliation of merely wounding their prey, or of missing it altogether. They chose a bazooka.

Environmental groups in Europe and America predictably went berserk. They felt stabbed in the back. After all, Indians are stereotypically idealized as stewards of the earth and kin to all its creatures. How could they go after

69

whales with something that looks like the kind of weapon Rambo used to wipe out armies of terrorists? More to the point of this book, were the Makah really maintaining a tradition, or trying to reinvent a long-dead identity in a hopelessly self-defeating way? Like the Sons of Italy and the United Daughters of the Confederacy, the Makah see themselves as embattled victims of cultural genocide. "They want us in the museum," declared a village elder involved in the hunt. "They'd rather we just said, 'Oh, the Makah were great whalers,' and leave it at that. They want us to have a dead culture. But it's been our way of life. We look at the ocean and we feel we not only have a legal right but a moral right to whale." In emotive cases like this, both the Indians and the environmentalists find themselves enmeshed in agonizing contradictions.

But the Makah quest, already the subject of semi-derisory national stories in the *New York Times Magazine* (August 9, 1998) and *U.S. News and World Report* (October 5, 1998), did not end there. The gray whales that the Makah intended to hunt migrate four thousand miles southward every fall from the Bering Sea to their calving grounds off Baja California. In the fall of 1998, a whole year after permission had been granted, the whaling crew practiced shooting its bazooka and other firearms at a barrel filled with water, kept their eyes peeled for the annual migration, and fended off Greenpeace and the media. These activities eventually became so wearing that at the beginning of December the crew's captain resigned, saying the job was taking up too much of his time. Nonetheless the Makah, who had been on the alert since September for the migrating

whales, chose a new captain and defended their plans in increasingly defiant terms. Although environmental groups
offered them money to give up the hunt, they vowed never
to sell out their cultural heritage.

A few days before Christmas, however, large numbers
of gray whales were spotted, not off the coast of Washington but in the vicinity of San Diego. An estimated 24,000 of
the world's largest mammals, many of them pregnant, had,
in the words of the *Seattle Times* (December 23, 1998), "apparently skirted the coast of the Pacific Northwest unno-
ticed" by the Makah, a flotilla of environmentalists, the
international media, and federal authorities who were keeping an eye on the situation.

In the days that followed, newspaper correspondence
columns in the Northwest could have run a contest for the
best suggestion as to what the Makah, outwitted for the
time being by their prey, should do next. One letter writer
suggested that instead of killing these large, gentle creatures, they might (despite having missed the boat this time)
offer peaceful whale-watching tours to raise money for the
tribe. "Let the Makahs show they can be brothers to the
whale," he piously concluded. Another correspondent suggested that rather than whales, the Makah should kill sea
lions, which are numerous enough on the Washington
coast to have become a pest, and use the ivory and pelts to
make authentic native clothing, which they could then market. The element of levity in the situation only strengthened
the resolve of the Makah to redeem themselves as hunters,
even though they would now have to wait until the whales
went north again in the spring. "We'll just have to get a

skinny one on the way back," one of the crew members de-clared matter-of-factly. And so they finally did, aided by a grant from the Commerce Department, after braving five more months of bad publicity and the disgust of environ-mental organizations.

The Makahs' dramatic effort to escape from the mu-seum—to prove that a cultural tradition from another age could be artificially revived at the end of the twentieth cen-tury—led to results that are easy to deplore or ridicule. If this is multiculturalism, many would say, then the whole concept needs to be rethought. It does indeed; that is one of the main points of this book. In reflecting on the fate of the Makah, however, we also need to remember that in less extreme forms, the inheritors of every culture, native or im-migrant, face essentially the same dilemma: whether to van-ish quietly into post-culturalism or defiantly reassert an antique distinctiveness.

But the term *multiculturalism* can also bear innocuous meanings that lead to much less contentious outcomes. It can encompass the inoffensive forms of nostalgia men-tioned earlier. It can mean simply emphasizing that not all the major contributions to American identity or civilization came from the British Isles, or from Europe. Or it can be no more than a generalized denunciation of prejudice. It can sometimes even mean the assertion of individual choice against the pressures of a group identity.

These watered-down senses of the word inspire little

controversy. "When I say multiculturalism has won, and that 'we are all multiculturalists now,'" Nathan Glazer explains, "I mean that we all now accept a greater degree of attention to minorities and women and their role in American history and social studies and literature classes in schools."[11] In *One Nation, After All*, a study of opinions and attitudes among the roughly three-quarters of Americans who consider themselves middle class, the sociologist Alan Wolfe declares his surprise that while Americans of every ethnic group oppose bilingualism, he finds powerful support for what he calls "benign multiculturalism"—"the principle that groups within the United States ought to be allowed to retain their distinctiveness, but only so long as they do so within an official culture that insists on the priority of the national community over subnational ethnic groups."[12]

In Wolfe's interviews, though, both the "official culture" and the "distinctiveness" of the ethnic groups have less to them than meets the ear.

> When we explained that we were not asking about language but culture, many said that was different: of course, we ought to respect other cultures. Teaching children respect for the many cultures brought to this country was variously described by our respondents as "very good," "real good," "important," "fine," "great," "really great," "neat," "superb," "helpful," and "necessary"; only a few said it was "harmful" or an example of "political correctness run amok." Even when challenged—on this question, we tried to be very chal-

73

lenging—people rarely backed down from their enthusiastic support for the idea. "Spend a week on this and a week on that, that way the person is full-rounded," said J. W. Cotton of Broken Arrow [Oklahoma]. Well, Maria intervened, some people say we need to stress the basics. "Like I said," he responded, "a week or two on each. I mean when you've got four or five months in school, I am sure you can sneak in a week or something. . . . There's room for fluffy stuff."

The main reason multiculturalism claims such a degree of popular support, Wolfe adds, is that contrary to the views of most of its academic theorists, "many of those who support it do so for universalistic rather than particularistic reasons." Just because, in the words of one respondent, "people are not very different. Deep down they are all the same," their "cultures" are all worthy of respect.[13] Instead of a challenge to liberal pluralism, "benign multiculturalism" becomes a restatement of it: people can choose to remind themselves of whatever ethnic identity pleases them best, almost as a hobby.

Although Wolfe does not say so, this bland, benevolent, almost eighteenth-century version of multiculturalism is more logical than it may seem to those familiar only with militant, particularistic forms. Except on the assumption of some universal human similarities, implying some form of equal human rights, why should I respect or even tolerate another culture and its members when their interests conflict with mine? Unless coupled with some acknowledgment of moral demands that transcend cultures, the assertion of strong ethnic identities leads not to peaceful coexistence but to unending conflicts and fantasies of genocide. That this discouraging conclusion has more than theoretical validity is evident today in many parts of the world, from Kosovo to Indonesia. At bottom, multiculturalism makes no sense without the prior assumption of ethical universalism, however unconscious.

What Wolfe's respondents ultimately mean by "American culture" or "Americanism" is not, as he appears to believe, something comparable to the relatively fixed ethnic identities toward which they express themselves so tolerantly. Rather it is the opposite of that kind of identity—a post-cultural order in which everyone's family portraits from the old country are welcome because the often combative, mutually incomprehensible ancestors they represent are safely dead. A true multiplicity of cultures existed during the long eras of conflict between ethnic and religious groups, of prejudices that had power to define the tribe by inclusion and exclusion. Today what most ordinary people who call for multiculturalism want is something more like post-culturalism: no conflict based on cultural factors, none of the sharp edges that cause bleeding.

The contradictions between academic multiculturalism and the realities of a mostly assimilated society have attracted other commentators besides Wolfe and Benjamin Barber, but few acknowledge the near-extinction of cultural differences in America. K. Anthony Appiah, for example, points out that "the way much discussion of recognition proceeds is strangely at odds with the individualist thrust of talk of authenticity and identity. If what matters about me is

75

my individual and authentic self, why is so much contemporary talk of identity about large categories—gender, ethnicity, nationality, 'race,' sexuality—that seem so far from individual?" Appiah, a Ghanaian professor of Afro-American studies and philosophy at Harvard, adds that "We make up selves from a tool kit of options made available by our culture and society. We do make choices, but we do not determine the options among which we choose."[14] This formulation may seem to blend the old ethnic determinism elegantly with the new individualism, but what happens after the tool kit becomes a whole shopping mall, when the "options" become so numerous that each is reduced (in the memorable words of Wolfe's Oklahoma informant) to a week or two of fluffy stuff?

David Hollinger repeats another caveat: "The assertion of group identities is so mainstream an activity that it is often observed that to affirm such subnational identities is an American ritual. The assertion of subnational particularisms is a well-established mode of finding one's way within American society." Nobody is left out of the game, not even WASPs who might once have boasted of ancestors begotten aboard the *Mayflower*: "So pronounced is this tendency in American life that even Anglo-Protestants, when they find themselves 'alone,' will often make a production out of dividing themselves into places of origin." This boutique variant of identity-shopping is fluffy stuff indeed. Hollinger concludes that ethnic identities are just as "constructed" as national ones, and that it makes "historical and practical sense for the United States to maintain its own public culture—constantly contested and critically revised, to be sure—against which the demands of various particularisms shall be obliged to struggle within a formal constitutional framework. . . . We can even be a people, so long as we remember that we are not a chosen people, or even the 'almost chosen people' invoked by Lincoln, but merely a people among peoples. . . ."[15] Like Appiah, Hollinger ends up uncomfortably asserting a liberal version of ethnic assimilation in which little is new but the extreme modesty with which the value of American nationality is asserted.

A major problem in understanding American identities today lies not in the humaneness of this equivocal ideal but in the frequent failure to notice how much *has* changed. As any reader of the classic immigrant autobiographies knows, the "public culture" that faced their authors in the heyday of immigration before World War I was far more definite and authoritative—more like a traditional culture in the anthropological sense—than anything that exists in America today. Now the only moral absolute with widespread popular sanction is what Wolfe calls the "Eleventh Commandment"—not to be judgmental. "To exclude, to condemn, is to judge, and middle-class Americans are reluctant to pass judgment on how other people act and think."[16]

In 1910, when nearly 15 percent of the population was foreign-born, a morally insistent Protestantism was the national religious norm. Benjamin Franklin and Ralph Waldo Emerson were the favorite national prophets; approved versions of Washington and Lincoln were the most important national heroes. Nearly every aspect of life, from dress and diet to child-rearing and burial practices, had its own set of norms derived from northern Europe as modified by American experience during a period of maximum national confidence. The public educational system, at the opposite extreme from multiculturalism or bilingualism, was designed to produce amnesia as quickly as possible about one's former life in a different country, especially if one's forebears were not Protestant.

Multiculturalists tend to overlook religion as a central determinant of culture. Despite legal equality and the constitutional separation of church and state, Catholic and Jewish (to say nothing of Hindu or Muslim) immigrants at the turn of the century faced momentous choices that were not merely religious: how far to go in maintaining a whole way of life and set of associations deeply alien to the native majority. Of my own grandparents, all immigrants or the children of immigrants, two had been brought up as Roman Catholics, one as a Jew, one as a Protestant. In America, only the Protestant continued to practice his religion (albeit in a more "American" version) after he became an adult. The national capital actually has a National Cathedral— Protestant Episcopal, designed by its architects to resemble Canterbury, but larger—that was begun shortly after the turn of the century and completed, with some embarrassment, in 1990. Today no one would dream of building such an edifice. The idea of a religiously based national moral consensus, like so many other formerly shared assumptions about how individuals should live their lives, now looks as archaic as the laws that once prevented East Asians from immigrating to the United States.

Although most Americans describe themselves as religious, belief and practice have become almost totally personal, subjective matters in which emotional receptiveness to others is the major virtue. Judgmentalism, flanked by its offspring insensitivity and hypocrisy, is the one unforgivable sin. Regardless of denomination, contemporary mainstream religion makes few other demands on the behavior or beliefs even of its adherents, let alone on non-members. Among Protestants, illness and therapy have tacitly replaced sin and repentance as guiding pastoral concepts. America's "cafeteria Catholics" violate the Vatican's commands on birth control and other matters of doctrine so routinely that few priests or bishops bother to make an issue of it. With religion as with ethnicity, intermarriage has become so common that "cultural" boundaries barely exist except for relatively isolated groups like Hasidic Jews or Old Order Amish.

"Every indication suggests that they will continue to impose their individualism on their religious beliefs rather than the other way around," Wolfe concludes of his survey population, echoing the findings in Robert N. Bellah's 1985 sociological classic *Habits of the Heart*. "When forced to choose between authority and freedom, most middle-class Americans are persuaded that the freedom they enjoy in their private lives is too appealing to be surrendered for the sake of abstract moral principles that do not seem fully in accord with how they want to lead their lives."[17] Insofar as multiculturalism means a wide choice of personal identities or "lifestyles"—shifting, temporary, overlapping—it faces scarcely any significant opposition in the United States at the beginning of the millennium. The multiculturalism of strong ethnic values and group solidarity maintained heroically against the pressures of a Eurocentric majority, on the other hand, is as dead in the real world as the nineteenth-century anthropology that gave rise to its basic concepts. In the university and elsewhere, this sort of multiculturalism represents the nostalgia of the left for an older world, the exact counterpart of conservative nostalgia for a small-town, Christian, pre–New Deal America that vanished long ago down the same historical drain.

"'Multicultural' is a good adjective," the philosopher Peter Caws insists: "it has a generous feel to it, it is welcoming, inclusive, embracing . . . an openness to the variety of human pursuits and achievements."[18] The most enthusiastic multiculturalists of all equate the sacredness of life with the sacredness of cultures. The idea of culture itself becomes quasi-religious, an object of faith and devotion. In a 1994 symposium entitled *Multiculturalism: Examining the Politics of Recognition,* edited by Amy Gutmann, the ecologist Steven Rockefeller expresses this conception at its most grandiose:

> It may be argued that human cultures are themselves like life forms. They are the products of natural evolutionary processes of organic growth. Each, in its own distinct fashion, reveals the way the creative energy of the universe, working through human nature in interaction with a distinct environment, has come to a unique focus. Each has its own place in the larger scheme of things, and each possesses intrinsic value quite apart from whatever value its traditions may have for other cultures.[19]

Problems arise, however, when one examines the assumptions underlying this formulation. First, what is it that one is respecting when one respects the "intrinsic value" of another culture? Something different from one's own inheritance, or an echo of something already familiar? If, like many young people in the 1960s, I find Buddhism admirable because of its emphases on peace and equality, am I embracing something genuinely "other" or merely finding confirmation for ideals I already hold? Or is the point of consistent multiculturalism, as Rockefeller implies, to honor those aspects of other cultures that really are "other," such as caste in traditional Hinduism, foot-binding in imperial China, *Bushido* (the warriors' code) in pre-1945 Japan?

As we have been seeing, the more practical question has to do with what features of a culture survive in the kind of society that is described as multicultural. If cultures are like life forms, they must eventually grow old and die, but few advocates of multiculturalism take this possibility into account. On the contrary, the philosopher Susan Wolf proudly describes the newfound immortality that old cultures have been enjoying since their discovery by such people as herself and her fellow parents in university communities:

Every time I go to the library with my children, I am presented with an illustration of how generations past have failed to recognize the degree to which our community is multicultural, and of how the politics of recognition can lead, and indeed is leading, to a kind of social progress. My children tend to gravitate toward the section with folk stories and fairy tales. They love many of the same stories that I loved as a child—Rapunzel, the Frog Prince, the Musicians of Bremen—but their favorites also include tales from Africa, Asia, Eastern Europe, and Latin America that were unavailable to me when I was growing up. . . . By having these books and by reading them, we come to recognize ourselves as a multicultural community and so to recognize and respect the members of that community in all our diversity.[20]

It goes without saying, however, that the books Professor Wolf has in mind are all in English, all published in the British Isles or North America, all written for an audience of English-speaking parents and children. The "culture" that produced these books for its own purposes is Western. As in the stereotypical economy of imperialism, only the raw materials come from Africa, Asia, or another poor region of the globe—fossil souvenirs, at least in the American context, rather than expressions of living cultural variation.

Sometimes this nostalgic memento-hunting takes even more poignant forms: for instance, the other as grandmother. Around 1990 Jenna Rosen and Marcia Delman of New York decided to manufacture a line of dolls representing grandmothers of different ethnic groups. As the magazine *Modern Maturity* explains, "The creators were mindful of the fact that grandmothers are historians, family storytellers who keep the rest of the clan aware of distant relatives and their real-life stories. Therefore, each of the dolls comes with a cassette tape of stories from Granny's youth, along with lullabies and folk songs. 'We're trying to achieve emotional and ethnic authenticity,' says Rosen. 'Our dolls do not replace the real thing, of course, but they evoke the warmth of a grandmother's unconditional love.'"[21] Judging by the costumes the dolls wear, these grandmothers (who range from pioneer Midwestern to African American to Jewish to Italian) all grew up in the nineteenth century. Apart from skin and hair color, their features are identical right down to their affectionate grins; the differences are only skin-deep. A gamut of meanings should be obvious: nostalgia for ethnic roots that have been wilting for an entire century now, eagerness for news about one's long-lost extended "clan," and a yearning for the love and emotional simplicity now associated with a child's relation not to its parents but to its grandmother. Multiculturalism never had a more transparent set of symbols.

We have come a long way from my Korean-American student, but perhaps not too far to see that her situation represents both hope and discouragement, and not only for her. On the one hand, liberty to choose one's way of life, openness to outside influences, and a secular equality are basic American values that much of the world yearns for. The freeing of individuals from the shackles of a regressive group identity is one of the most powerful and constructive ideals in all of history. On the other hand, what is lost when everyone speaks the same vernacular, learns about the world from the same television programs, feels the same indifference toward any impersonal sources of value, and even nibbles on the same mixture of once-defining foods?

Many of the products of post-culturalism seem destitute of weight or depth because they lack the grounding and definition that real cultures, with real demands and convictions, used to provide. In a post-cultural state, vastly more depends on individual tastes and choices than in traditional cultures. Some individuals find hitherto unsuspected opportunities for shallowness, conformity, or narcissism, while others discover ways to express themselves more completely than they could have before. Paradoxically, the flattening out of cultures, by reducing group-based differences, leads simultaneously to greater individuality and greater homogenization. (This paradox will be the subject of Chapter 4.)

Most individuals in North America today have so many "cultural" options that the strong identities on which multiculturalism depends have become museum pieces, tiles in an ancient mosaic whose colors and design have faded beyond recall. What happens, for example, when representatives of two sophisticated, wholly distinct ethnic groups from different continents merge their lives in a post-cultural setting? The November 2, 1997, *New York Times* carried a review of a book about interfaith marriages—an old subject on which many volumes have been written since at least the 1940s. One quintessentially post-cultural sentence in this review, more succinct, touching, and at the same time ironic than the account in the book itself, will carry us efficiently to the next chapter. It was about a couple in Hawaii who had married and hyphenated their names as Schandler-Wong. She was Jewish; he was Chinese. Here is the sentence: "When Alvin Wong decided to convert to Judaism, his assimilationist parents were overjoyed by this proof that their son—from whom they had calculatedly withheld instruction in the use of chopsticks—was now really an American."

Chapter Three

Intermarriage and the 2050 Fallacy

In the beginning was John Smith. White, Anglo-Saxon, Protestant, with his perfect proto-American name, he wandered into the Virginia forest and was captured by Indians of Powhatan's Confederacy in December 1607, seven months after the founding of Jamestown. When he was on the point of being executed with stone clubs, the twelve-year-old daughter of the Indian emperor saved his life ("got his head into her armes," as Smith later wrote, "and laid her owne upon his, to save him from death"), and he was allowed to go free. The following year Smith in turn saved the Jamestown colony from starving to death. But in 1609 he left Virginia forever and went back to England. A few years later the Princess Matoaka, known to history by the nickname Pocahontas ("playful one"), married a colonist named John Rolfe, was baptized Rebecca, and likewise departed for England, where the king and queen made much of her. In London her portrait was painted in court dress while she held up an ostrich plume. Alas, she soon died of smallpox, aged about twenty-two, and was buried at Gravesend on the banks of the Thames. In 1962 Philip Young, a literary scholar, estimated that she had two million descendants.[1] For centuries blue-blooded Virginians have boasted of being her posterity.

But everyone knows she should have married Captain John Smith and stayed in the New World. If the two of them had succeeded to her father's power, the history of English-speaking America would have gone the way it was meant to from the start. The Indians would not have disappeared from the land; there would have been no African slavery. Even the forests would still be standing. Two races and civilizations would have blended peacefully, seamlessly. The world would have stayed new. Or so the Anglo-American creation myth has it, our own version of paradise lost.

Intermarriage—its temptations, its opportunities, its mortal dangers—has been a fascination of the American mind and story from the very beginning. It has always been controversial, opposed by those who believe in maintaining group identity, generally supported by those of universalistic views. (Of course, few people marry to satisfy a social theory.) Shakespeare's *Othello*, which can be interpreted to support either point of view, had its first performance three years before the founding of Jamestown.

To start with, what counts as intermarriage? Even here

consensus is hard to find. The most common meaning used to be marriage between members of two different religions. In the nineteenth century, when theology meant more, it might even describe marriage between a Methodist and a Presbyterian. Certainly unions between Catholics and Protestants were examples of intermarriage—generally frowned on by both sets of relatives. Then there are ethnic, or cultural, intermarriages. Does it count when a WASP marries someone of German descent? It certainly did once; remember that until Hitler's time the term *race*, with its implication of momentous difference, was often used casually in English to describe any well-defined ethnic group. ("He was a credit to the Italian race," the octogenarian shortstop Phil Rizzuto told a television interviewer the day Joe DiMaggio died.)

Is it intermarriage when a white Protestant and a Mexican American marry in the Southwest? There you have both religion and ethnicity, though not necessarily race in the modern sense. Today, while none of these usages is entirely obsolete, the most common meaning of intermarriage is marriage between members of two clearly defined (at least in the mind of the speaker) races: black and white, white and Asian, Asian and black. . . . The marriage of John Rolfe and Pocahontas was intermarriage by any of these definitions, but most cases are not so clear-cut.

Why has the term changed its connotations over time? Largely, no doubt, because belonging to, or marrying into, a particular religion or ethnic group is so much less important in American life than it once was, less decisive in determining most people's futures or outlook. Also, perhaps, because racial intermarriage in the modern sense is so much more common than it used to be. While marriages between whites and Indians were sometimes (by no means always) approved of, in 1900 thirty states or future states had laws against unions between whites and blacks, and in many cases also between whites and Asians. The Supreme Court finally declared the last of these statutes unconstitutional in 1967 in the sublimely named case of *Loving v. Virginia.* "At some point," John J. Miller points out, "intermarriage . . . becomes simply marriage. When an Irish American married an Italian American seventy-five years ago, it was probably a big deal in the neighborhood. But no more. In the future, everyone will have a Korean grandmother."[2]

A few statistics may be useful here, though it should be kept in mind that published figures are rarely up to date, suffer from ambiguous definitions of the status of the affected parties, and are sometimes inconsistent with one another. As I indicated earlier, about 40 percent of Hispanics born in the United States and 50 percent of native-born Asian Americans now marry outside their own ethnic groups. (There are considerable variations among particular nationality groups in both categories.) American Indians, at 53 percent, have the highest intermarriage rate. In New York City, according to a 1991 study of marriage records, the proportion of exogamous Hispanics was well over half. According to the Census Bureau's figures for 1997, over 29 percent of *all* Hispanic marriages (including those of immigrants who were married before they came to this country) are with non-Hispanics, a number that has been rising from census to census. People of Asian descent are not included separately in the 1997 table, but the 1990 census showed that 30 percent of all Asian marriages were already with non-Asians.

As for marriages between black and white Americans, historically the greatest taboo, the bureau gave them in 1997 as 7.5 percent of all black marriages; the number had nearly doubled since 1980 and was six times what it had been in 1960. (Since the 1970s, black men have been almost twice as likely to marry white women as black women to marry white men.) Marriages between a black spouse and a spouse who was neither white nor black—in most cases of Asian descent—accounted for about another 1.5 percent of all black marriages. The higher their income or education, the more likely black Americans are to marry people who are not black. Perhaps the most confounding statistic is that according to the 1990 census only 53 percent of married black Americans under the age of twenty-five were married to other blacks. The total number of interracial couples in 1997 as defined by the Census Bureau was 1,264,000, about 2.3 percent of all married couples in the country. This last number has likewise doubled since 1980 and is eight and a half times what it was in 1960. The trends here are much more important than the actual figures, which are almost always out of date before they can be tabulated and published.[3]

The Census Bureau does not ask questions about religion, but Jewish intermarriage has been compulsively studied by Jewish groups. The most extensive survey ever taken of American Jews, the National Jewish Population Survey of

1990, reported that 52 percent of Jews married since 1985 had married non-Jews.[4] This figure has been disputed on methodological grounds, but few doubt that the actual number is at least close to it. Catholic intermarriage is somewhat less studied but, like all other categories of exogamy, has been increasing. According to a 1993 examination of earlier studies, among practicing Catholics born in the 1950s about a quarter of the men and a third of the women married non-Catholics. The proportion was much higher for people who had been brought up as Catholics but no longer practiced their religion.[5] As for marriages between different branches of Protestants, hardly anyone still regards them as intermarriage at all now that long-established denominations themselves are merging right and left.

What should we make of these figures? Much has been written about the acceptance of the children of mixed marriages within the communities of both their parents, with treatment varying dramatically depending on many factors. According to Paul R. Spickard, who studied several varieties of intermarriage exhaustively in the 1980s, the children of marriages between Japanese Americans and whites were often ostracized by both groups until intermarriage became more common in the 1950s, when—finally, predictably—assimilation on one side and a decline of anti-Japanese prejudice on the other began to ease matters for the children as well as their parents.[6]

Now that native-born Japanese Americans are just as likely to marry white Americans as members of their own ethnic group, the problem of children who are ambiguous—between two cultures in a sense, but really outside both—is less of a problem, unless you consider the loss of relatively pure identity on either side to be another, different problem. Ethnic exclusiveness has broken down in both groups, but most people would not mourn its passing. It declined through a myriad of individual decisions, marital choices that were certainly not forced on either partner by his or her own culture. Quite the contrary: a drastic reduction of cultural authority on both sides was necessary for intermarriage to reach such dimensions. Once it becomes normal, intermarriage among ethnic groups does more than anything else to make the transition from multiculturalism (the mutual toleration of several or many distinct cultures in the same society) to post-culturalism irreversible.

One of the children Spickard interviewed grew up in Brooklyn as the daughter of a Japanese-American father from California and a Jewish New Yorker. When Joy Nakamura began college in the late 1960s, she underwent a predictable identity crisis that was made more intense by the fashionable ethnic assertiveness of some of her classmates. Was she white or Asian, Japanese or Jewish, an American or a victim of America? "I was desperately trying to find myself as an Asian-American woman, but I was not succeeding," she wrote to the author in 1974. Part of the difficulty was that her newfound Japanese-American friends expressed hostility toward whites. A black friend also told her: "You must decide if you are yellow, or if you are white. Are you part of the Third World, or are you against it?" At the same time she argued with her white boyfriend about racial issues.

Finally she decided, "I do not feel guilty about not recognizing my Asianness; I have already done so. I have just readjusted my guilt feelings about ignoring my Jewish half. . . . My uniqueness separates me from everyone else. This is a scary idea. I am all alone. I cannot even find group solidarity from a gathering of Eurasians; we are all too different." Although Spickard assures his readers that "she remains well adjusted to both her ethnic identities," the entire story demonstrates that in such cases the whole idea of ethnic identity, real or artificial, has become a curse.[7] What is at stake here, besides the happiness of an individual, is an abstract solidarity whose defects clearly outweigh its advantages. Would matters be different if a religion, a set of beliefs and commitments that is to some extent separable from a particular ethnic identity, were also at stake? What if the emphasis in Joy's case were not on Japaneseness or Jewishness but rather on Judaism?

Consider the Schandler-Wong family mentioned at the end of the last chapter. The idea of Chinese-American Jews in Hawaii, or Jewish-Chinese Americans, is exotic and appealing, partly because it bridges so much of the earth and also because, as the bride's mother said to the groom, "you come from the *other* Old World civilization."[8] An alliance between two such ancient, erudite, and well-defined traditions seems to have a special significance. Is that significance "multicultural"? Well, Gabrielle Glaser, who tells the Schandler-Wong story in *Strangers to the Tribe*, certainly thinks so. But the moment during which both traditions survive in a vivid, graceful embrace may not last for longer than a dance or two. Chinese ethnicity is obviously diluted by intermarriage, particularly when the Chinese-American groom converts to a non-Chinese religion. To substitute the word *enriched* for *diluted* makes the same point even more forcefully: for Chinese or any other ethnicity to be improved by being mixed with something different implies that it was incomplete in itself. A mixture that could never have occurred before emigration in either of the two cultures whose representatives are intermarrying may seem to merge them in the offspring. Actually it divides the offspring decisively from both cultures and makes them irrevocably post-cultural Americans.

Jewish identity differs from an ethnicity in that historically it depends on having a Jewish mother who transmits a set of convictions and a repertory of rituals to her children. So the fate of that identity in such a marriage is especially instructive about the trajectory by which multiculturalism rapidly turns into post-culturalism. Trudy Schandler married Alvin Wong in 1975. Their son Ari was born in 1980, their daughter Shaaroni in 1982. After some inner conflict, their mother decided not to raise them kosher, a decision that Gabrielle Glaser presents as a victory of enlightened tolerance over tradition.

As she tells it, the family has made a virtue of adapting Jewishness to the eclectic, East-meets-West-and-then-some life of Hawaii, where nearly two-thirds of the population is of Asian or Pacific extraction. Ari's bar mitzvah dinner was held at a Chinese restaurant; Shaaroni wore a muumuu to her bat mitzvah. "And so it is," the author writes, "that Ari Wong feels 'a hundred percent Jewish.' 'It's totally cool,' he says. At sixteen, he loves his name and its reflection of both family histories."[9] His only reservation comes at Passover, when the family abstains from rice, a staple of his favorite Chinese meals. (Once again, culture in America comes down to food.) Otherwise, apart from minor difficulties and misunderstandings, parents and children seem perfectly adapted to their unusual heritage—in fact, an ideal American family whose experiences could be the basis for a thoroughly familiar kind of television series.

"Transcending one's culture of origin does not mean turning one's back on it," Peter Caws points out. "We live in a world that is irreversibly plural where culture is concerned, but a basis for the harmonious coexistence of cultures can be found in the mutual sharing of what is convergent . . . and in a mutual respect for what is divergent. . . ."[10] What soon happens to the sharers and to the culture shards they share is post-culturalism. The Schandler-Wongs, says the book, "have taken a bit from here and there. They have woven Jewish, Chinese, and Hawaiian cultures into their home like a bird building a nest from twigs, mud, and foil."[11] They like living in Hawaii, the most ethnically mixed and intermarried state in the Union, precisely because it offers so many cultural choices—bits and pieces from everywhere—and makes so few insistent cultural demands. For the twigs, mud, and foil that birds use to build are after all only remnants, bits that fell off something else. Any influence that Jewish, Chinese, or Hawaiian cultures have on this family is purely residual, a matter of individual preference, and individual preference is the opposite of culture as traditionally understood. We have come a long way from Ruth Benedict.

Unless the Schandler-Wongs and other families like

them rediscover Judaism in its traditional exclusiveness, their sense of being Jewish seems unlikely to outlast the convert's children. But that exclusiveness, the conviction of being a uniquely chosen tribe, is precisely what post-culturalism finds most offensive. The result is that, as Alan Wolfe has pointed out, the sharp edges of definition get worn off every religion. What survives best is a vague feeling of universal beneficence that adapts itself to whatever social, moral, or philosophical views are dominant at any given time.

Historians of American religion from de Tocqueville to the present have often pointed out that pantheism, the assertion that everything is God, has a particular attraction in democratic, egalitarian societies. No one and nothing is left out of the primordial unity; no moral or metaphysical distinctions have to be made. A religion that demands much more of its adherents, especially one that violates Wolfe's "eleventh commandment" of non-judgmentalism, finds itself controversial because it constantly threatens to rock someone out of the boat. Despite its sometimes intolerant history, Christianity, like Islam, is a universalistic religion of conversion and can adapt not only to cultures other than the one in which it originated, but to a non-judgmental, post-cultural, intermarrying age. An explicitly non-universal religion like Judaism, which depends heavily on lineal descent, has more difficulty flourishing in such an environment.

Jews in contemporary America are faced with the unattractive choice of either asserting their particularity by seceding from the larger society, as the ultra-Orthodox do, or of surrendering many traditional aspects of Jewishness to the prevailing Zeitgeist. Attempts to compromise these two positions, to adapt in part while retaining a durable minimum of Jewish identity, have not been very successful, judging from such indicators as intermarriage rates, the percentage of "mixed" children who are raised as Jews, or the health of non-Orthodox Jewish religious organizations. Jack Wertheimer, provost of the Jewish Theological Seminary, estimates that the proportion of American Jews who are Orthodox, now only about 6 percent, may well grow dramatically, partly because their birthrate greatly exceeds that of non-Orthodox Jews:

> This fecundity will have noticeable effects on the larger Jewish community within a generation or two, particularly since, unlike the situation earlier in this century, the "retention" rate for Orthodox children has recently become very high. They tend overwhelmingly to marry other Jews, usually other Orthodox Jews, and usually at a young age (thereby further assuring high rates of fertility). By contrast, non-Orthodox Jews are barely replacing themselves, and their rates of intermarriage with non-Jews range from 30 to over 50 percent.[12]

Of course, as Wertheimer makes clear, this prediction depends on Orthodox Jews continuing to resist the usual American patterns of assimilation and intermarriage.

In the Schandler-Wong marriage, the bride had been prepared by her upbringing and her parents' outlook on life

97

to marry a non-Jew. As her mother told the author, "My children were never brought up to be concerned with anything but the person, whether he be black or yellow or red or green. We've been very blessed by having friends of all races who respect our way of worship, just as we respect theirs." Living in Asheville, North Carolina, far from Northern centers of Jewish solidarity, the family had adapted. Mrs. Schandler had heard complaints from other Jewish parents whose children married non-Jews, but she found them hard to understand. "I ask them: Are you willing to give up your son or daughter because of this? Aren't you happy to have another member of the family? What about your grandchildren? Do you want to alienate them? Look at the person first; that's my advice."[13]

This universalistic individualism—the sense that an individual's race, culture, or religion has almost no importance compared to the individual himself—is utterly typical of how Americans evaluate one another. When they talk about respecting cultural diversity, they really mean that cultural differences have become thin enough to ignore, or more positively that group identities *should* be disregarded as much as possible, except perhaps as a form of local color. Your child, in fact any sympathetic individual, is more important than the solidarity of any group.

"To confine the development of one's identity within the variables of any single culture seems to me to be a wanton neglect of the vast riches that are available in the world," declares Peter Caws.[14] Who would wish Mrs. Schandler or her family to be different from what they are? Their openness and courage are enormous virtues. The next chapter will have more to say about the particular kind of individualism that underlies them. Here the point is simply that Mrs. Schandler's admirable receptiveness toward people of other backgrounds runs contrary to the exclusiveness that kept the Jews going as an identifiable minority for two thousand years in the Diaspora. A conviction that all faiths have equal value may well be fatal to the preservation of Jewish religious or cultural distinctiveness in an intermarrying land where most people are not Jews. Why go to all the trouble of keeping a kosher kitchen unless you believe that God chose the Jews to be his special tribe, different from other peoples? A family among those in Gabrielle Glaser's mixed marriages might possibly do it for a single generation out of habit or ethnic loyalty, or more likely keep up less demanding customs like the annual seder, but scarcely longer.

"I leave to others more trained in Jewish learning the historic and vexing question, 'Who is a Jew?'" Glaser announces modestly. "Are these intermarried Jews, whose children celebrate Hanukkah, Passover, and Christmas, real or ersatz Jews? It is not for me to say."[15] Perhaps the only eventuality that could preserve Jewish identity among the non-Orthodox would be a powerful, enduring outbreak of anti-Semitism, a calamity that fortunately has little prospect of coming about.

It is revealing that the 1970s and '80s, when Jewish intermarriage was growing by leaps and bounds, were the very decades during which the building of Holocaust memorials and museums, together with the teaching of courses about the destruction of Europe's Jews, took on a quasi-religious fervor. Every willing survivor is to be tape-recorded as a means of bearing permanent witness to a time when being Jewish, or even partly Jewish, was a matter of life and death. Starting in the 1960s, terms such as *ghetto, diaspora,* and later *Holocaust,* which had once carried exclusively Jewish associations, gradually became available for use by other groups that had suffered from prejudice. Holocaust museums themselves seldom remained limited to the sufferings of Jews; instead they inclined more and more to function as warnings against prejudice in general. Postculturalism turns everything, whether sacred or profane, into twigs and foil from which any breed of bird can try to build a nest.

The demand for cosmetic nose surgery is in steep decline at the turn of the millennium, and the once great Catskill resorts are dying. Yiddish, though taught in the growing number of university Jewish Studies programs, is all but dead as a cradle tongue. Like so many of Americans' ancestral heritages, Jewish religion and Jewish ethnicity alike are rapidly becoming one of several or many branches on the family tree, something to remember fondly now and then but a long way back, not a set of beliefs or practices that distinguishes those who have them in any important way from Americans with no Jewish ancestry.

On May 17, 1998, the forty-fourth anniversary of the Supreme Court's *Brown v. Board of Education* decision, the *Washington Post Magazine* published with great fanfare autobiographical articles by three writers under the collective title "Middle Ground: Growing Up Across Racial and Cultural Divides." "There's a subtle revolution underway in America today," the magazine enthusiastically headlined its symposium—"a revolution in which biculturalism, in one form or another, is becoming the norm." The *Post* assumed, without thinking much about it, that "bicultural" children have more in common with one another, regardless of their origins, than any of them has with supposedly "monocultural" Americans. Not so subtly conflating racial and cultural mixtures, the editors described this revolution as a "personal and political shift." The three authors themselves, as one might expect, were more ambivalent. Their accounts are worth examining because of what they show, from what are in fact three very different standpoints, about the actual lives of recent immigrants and their children.

Malcolm Gladwell is the son of a British father and a Jamaican mother who was "not black," he explains, "but brown," of mixed ancestry. His parents met at the University of London in the middle fifties, felt comfortable together by virtue of both being middle class, and soon fell in love. Despite his father's family's objections to the match on racial grounds, they soon married. "It was hard," Gladwell writes, "for white to marry black in the 1950s because mixed marriages were so unmistakably political. For my father, though, I think it was easy. The surest way to commit a revolutionary act, after all, is not to perceive what you are doing as revolutionary."

Political approaches *cultural* in ambiguity today, and what Gladwell means by it here is less than clear. Equating it with *revolutionary* only makes its significance more obscure. Normally a revolutionary act brings about some change in the law or the state, or at least in custom. Interracial marriages have never been illegal in Britain. Since the 1950s they have become much more common, in part simply because Britain has so many more non-white residents than it did then. But the senior Mr. Gladwell seems to have had no intention of being political, let alone revolutionary. The article makes it clear that all he wanted was to marry the woman he loved, for the most normal and ordinary of reasons. He sounds, in fact, a great deal like Mrs. Schandler.

The vocabulary his son uses to make private action seem public deflects attention from the really striking part of the story, a migration in two stages. First the family moved to Canada, where Malcolm Gladwell grew up. As an adult he moved by himself to the United States. The view of life in his article seems in some ways more Canadian than American. For reasons perhaps having to do with their own precarious sense of national identity, Canadian academics and journalists often go out of their way to contrast the United States unfavorably with their own country. In recounting his upbringing, Gladwell adverts briefly to this Canadian habit as it relates to his own understandable obsession with race:

> Back then, "race" and all that it connoted was something uniquely American. I would read the old *Life* magazine every week and see pictures of civil rights marches, or black protestors, or Angela Davis with her sky-high Afro, and my only thought was how foreign it

all was. . . . Atlanta, I knew, was steamy and humid and fetid, and all I could think about was that it was the racism that was making the air so thick down there. The air was not thick in Canada. It was dry and light, blown fresh across the Great Lakes.

For motives he never explains, Gladwell left the fresh air behind, came to work for the *Washington Post*, and is now a staff writer for the *New Yorker*. Living in a land of mixtures, however, did not make him feel comfortable.

His problem as he defines it is not cultural. For an observant man of mixed parentage who has lived in three countries, he has surprisingly little to say about culture. Perhaps he and others in his situation talk compulsively about race because the cultures of immigrants change so rapidly, and they feel the need of a more durable language for their sense of alienation. The collectivity they left behind with such mixed feelings is referred to as a race, but it could be any group identity. Whatever the reason, Gladwell expresses his discomfort entirely in racial language.

"I go back and forth now between my two sides," he tells us. "If you mix black and white, you don't obliterate those categories; you merely create a third category, a category that demands, for its very existence, an even greater commitment to nuances of racial taxonomy." This melancholy thought—that his parents' "revolutionary act" only intensified the problems of racial identity—seems to suggest that more is lost than gained by intermarriage. Letting go of racial identity altogether seems not to occur to the younger Gladwell, even as an ultimate social goal. "Racial intermar-

riage solves one problem in the first generation, only to create another in the next—a generation that cannot ignore
difference the way their parents did." This conclusion raises
an obvious question: if the politically naive parents could
see beyond racial differences in England in the 1950s, why
do the sophisticated children have so much trouble doing
so in a more enlightened time? Here the perception of "difference," usually celebrated today as a virtue, seems to be
little more than a prisoner's awareness of the bars on his
window. The parents, some readers will inevitably feel, were
wiser and more future-oriented than the children.

Unlike Malcolm Gladwell, Eric Liu, author of a widely
reviewed memoir called *The Accidental Asian,* from which
his *Post Magazine* article was excerpted, is a native-born
American; nor is he the product of a mixed marriage,
though his children are. Both his parents were semi-assimi-
lated Chinese immigrants who, like the Wongs and the
Schandlers, quickly grasped the American principle "that
their children were entitled to mix or match, as they saw fit,
whatever aspects of whatever cultures they encountered."
Married to a white woman, their son now thinks he has assimilated all the way, a conclusion to which he brings the
ambivalence verging on self-loathing of the upwardly mobile intellectual who in some moods fears that by "acting
white," as his accusers put it, he has betrayed his ethnic
roots.

I have assimilated. I am of the mainstream. In many
ways I fit the psychological profile of the so-called
banana: imitative, impressionable, rootless, eager to

please. . . . Yet I'm not sure that what I did was so cut and dried as "becoming white." I plead guilty to certain charges: achieving, learning the ways of the upper middle class, distancing myself from radicals of any hue. But having confessed, I still do not know my crime.

What, after all, *is* the crime? Betraying an identity implies that one had the power to maintain it, and furthermore that it was worth maintaining. But was either of those things true? "I may have been born a Chinese baby, but it would have taken unremitting reinforcement, by my parents and by myself, for me to have remained Chinese." The issue is not whether being Chinese was inherently worthwhile, but whether being Chinese was a real or desirable option for someone born in the United States during the second half of the twentieth century. "I have neglected my ancestral heritage," he admits. "Yes, I can speak some Mandarin and stir-fry a few easy dishes. I have been to China and know something of its history. Still, I could never claim to be Chinese at the core."

Like my Korean-American student who described herself as "American to the core," Liu experiences the peremptory demand of nostalgic multiculturalism—you must maintain your parents' identity—as oppressive. Assimilation, finally, is both an unavoidable fact and a victory. Of course the process he describes is more tolerant than assimilation in the heyday of immigration around 1900, when the Mandarin and the stir-fry would have been confined to the family kitchen. Really he means integration into an order where, as he says, culture is a voluntary matter of

mixing and matching. The common accusation of "becoming white" is inaccurate, he writes; reducing such a complicated adaptation to hackneyed racial terms hides more than
it reveals.

Finally, Liu's story is an optimistic one, in some ways
resembling the immigrant autobiographies of the early
twentieth century. Not realizing how familiar this part of his
conclusion would have sounded eighty years ago, he asserts
that the time has come "to conceive of assimilation as more
than a series of losses—and to recognize that what is lost is
not necessarily sacred." His own life so far, as he examines
it, has been a success. More significantly for his readers, it
points to something new in the world, something for which
he has no name—what I have called post-culturalism.

> Something new is emerging from the torrent, in my
> case and the many millions like it. Something undevel-
> oped, speaking the unformed tongue of an unformed
> nation . . . Whatever it is that I am becoming, is it any
> less authentic for being an amalgam? . . . What it
> means to be American—in spirit, in blood—is some-
> thing far more borrowed and commingled than any-
> thing previous generations ever knew. Alongside the
> pain of migration, then, and the possibility, there is this
> truth: America is white no longer, and it will never be
> white again.

Things have changed after all: immigrants who "assimilate" are no longer joining a culture as their predecessors
did. That discovery can be deeply unsettling (and not only

for immigrants) but also potentially liberating for Americans of every color, language, and ancestral land of origin. Of course the classic immigrant autobiographies also emphasized that the loss of an old identity could be painful, and that something (in their case, usually patriotism toward an idealized nation of immigrants) must be found to take its place. When culture goes, what do we use for a map to find our way through a new life in an "unformed nation"? In a post-cultural age, this problem too is not for immigrants alone.

Meri Nana-Ama Danquah, the *Post Magazine*'s third writer, came from Ghana to Washington, D.C., in the early 1970s with her parents. The family always intended to return home but somehow never did. In their attitude toward America, her parents were the opposite of Liu's. "In consideration of our imminent departure," she says, "assimilation was frowned upon. My parents tried to fan the flames of our culture within me, in hopes they would grow into a raging fire and burn fully any desire I had to become an American." They insisted that she go on speaking Ga, their native language, and refused to answer her in English.

She was only six when she moved to the United States, a natural age to learn a new language with comparatively little effort. Instead she seems to have floated continually a few feet above the earth, never able to decide who she was or where she lived. Her childhood was made even more complicated by American racial divisions. As a black African, to what elements in American life would she assimilate, if she assimilated at all? For years she tried to speak English with the accent of her black American friends. But "there was a curtain of sheer hostility hanging between black Americans and black Africans." Black children were crueler to her than anyone else; they were always telling her to go back to Africa. She studied Spanish and made Hispanic friends. If she could not fit in with black Americans, perhaps she could identify with them. As an adult she moved to Los Angeles with its myriad of shifting languages, cultures, identities, a place where she feels she finally found herself.

"I have housed many identities inside the one person I presently call myself, a person I know well enough to admit that I don't know at all. Like a chameleon, I am ever-changing, able to blend without detection into the colors and textures of my surroundings, a skill developed out of a need to belong, a longing to be claimed." According to her account, being claimed and belonging never really happened. Although she has now lived in this country for twenty-four years, she has never been naturalized and today thinks of herself as a citizen of the world.

Many readers will find this story depressing, but it does not quite end there. As people so often do, Meri Nana-Ama Danquah had a child. (The article significantly does not mention the girl's father.) Korama, now six, the same age her mother was when she came to America, sounds an altogether more American sort of American child, with none of the problems her mother had in growing up. Of course every child has her own problems; the point in the article is that Korama's seem to be of a wholly different kind. As children will do, she revealed to a school friend that her mother's favorite television show was "The X-Files." As par-

ents often are in such situations, her mother was embar-
rassed and told her so. Then it came out that Korama's
friend Hugo had said that only an alien would prefer that
program. To Korama, living in Los Angeles, an alien was a
creature from outer space. "Are you an alien?" she demanded.

The chasm that opens between immigrant parents and
their native-born children is usually narrated from the
child's point of view. Here for once we have the parent's.
"For a moment," Meri says of her daughter, "her stare was
as disempowering as those of the American children whom
I had encountered as a child, her questions as offensive. I
wanted to arm myself against the pain of being reminded
that I was 'other.' I wanted to beg that little girl before me to
try, to just try to accept—if not love—me for who I was, the
way I was, no matter how different that seemed from the
way she was." The self-dramatization and self-pity wrapped
in the jargon of multiculturalism ("disempowering," "offensive," "'other'") do not conceal a perfectly understandable
feeling of alienation from one's offspring. "But I knew I
didn't have to," she adds, "because she already did." When
daughter asks mother if she will always be an alien, mother
thinks for the first time of becoming an American citizen.

Whose story is this? Mother and daughter, two little
girls, have opposite experiences. The mother, amputated
from the past, spends her whole life (but remember that she
is still a young woman) searching unsuccessfully for something to take its place. She calls herself a citizen of the
world because she feels at home nowhere. The daughter is
a little post-cultural American. Each sees the other through

the prism of stereotypes. But the reader unavoidably ends up feeling that the daughter represents the future her mother should have had.

The first thing that stands out when one reads these three accounts together is how different they all are. From Eric Liu's slightly baffled optimism to Meri Danquah's sense of permanent alienation to Malcolm Gladwell's insistence on race, the writers have no more in common than any three well-educated Americans chosen at random. Perhaps that has something to do with the fact that, like my Korean-American student, none of them is really bicultural. Biculturalism implies two distinct cultures that the same person inhabits—in the *Washington Post*'s words—across divides. Not one of these authors comes close to living such a life. As Liu makes clearest of the three, the disappearance of distinct cultures with visible divides is precisely what makes life and identity so confusing. Learning to stir-fry easy dishes and speak a little Chinese suggests the mild loyalty to an ancestral heritage that most Americans sometimes feel; it has nothing to do with seriously inhabiting a culture. As for the other two writers, reasserting a long-ignored racial identity or remaining a citizen of a childhood homeland to which one never returns is a nostalgic symptom not of biculturalism but of post-cultural vertigo in people who have had to live with too many ambiguities. The *Post* was right to sense a "revolution" in the relation of Americans to culture and cultures. In trying to assimilate it to the conventional multiculturalist model, however, the editors overlooked much of what their three authors were actually saying.

It has become a commonplace, an article of faith, even a truism that the American population grows more diverse every year. This assertion has been used both to promote private tolerance and to justify a wide range of public policies, from affirmative-action preferences to multicultural education to bilingual government services. What exactly does it mean to say that America is more diverse than it used to be? Usually that the proportion of ethnic minorities—narrowly defined as persons who are not of European descent—is rising.

Journalists and academics frequently announce that minorities in this sense will soon constitute, or even that they already constitute, a majority of the population. This claim has been reinforced by exaggerated reporting of Census Bureau projections for the year 2050. With that curious propensity of "race" and "culture" to impersonate each other as if they were interchangeable terms, what is believed of one must be equally true of the other. If the population is less white than it used to be, it must be more alien to the American culture that was. If "culture" is changing, the population must be less white than it was. This whole set of assumptions seems to be shared not only by people who think other cultures should be preserved but also, more surprisingly, by people who believe in assimilation.

In March 1996 the Census Bureau issued projections of U.S. population by race for a succession of years ending in 2050. A January 2000 revision carried them more speculatively forward to 2100. These projections came in three "series," depending on assumptions about population growth over the period. In the lowest series, assuming a decline in birthrates and immigration, the population in 2050 would be 313,546,000. The highest series, making opposite assumptions about birth and immigration rates, produced a U.S. population in 2050 of 552,757,000—standing room only. The one that the bureau felt most confident about was the "middle series," which predicted a population in 2050 of 403,687,000. It was on the basis of this series that the bureau issued its widely but often inaccurately reported breakdown of the future population by race.

The Office of Management and Budget arbitrarily uses five major categories to define the racial makeup of American residents: white, black/African American, American Indian/Alaska Native, Asian, and Native Hawaiian/Pacific Islander. (Following earlier practice, the last two categories are usually combined in census reports as Asian/Pacific Islander.) Each individual answering the census is required to choose a racial identification. Until the 2000 census, respondents could select only one; now they are permitted to check off more than one "race" from a complicated menu. Despite the large and rapidly growing number of people with mixed parentage, however, the Census Bureau has persistently refused to introduce a "Mixed Race" category, something that civil rights groups vehemently oppose. How persons who choose more than one race will be identified in future reports is likely to remain a matter of lasting controversy.

In September 1999 the bureau estimated that of the 273,401,000 people then living in the United States, 82.3

percent were white, 12.8 percent black, .9 percent American Indian or Alaskan Native, and 4 percent Asian/Pacific Islander. If we jump forward to 2050, the bureau estimates that the white proportion will shrink to 74.9 percent, the black proportion grow to 14.7 percent, Asians and Pacific Islanders more than double to 9.3 percent, and Indians/Alaskan Natives hold almost steady at 1.1 percent. These racial changes are significant but far from overwhelming. No group changes its rank order, and whites remain an enormous majority. (Even in 2100, whites will be 70.7 percent.)

It was this last part that got so widely misreported. In addition to race, the Census Bureau also keeps track of the Hispanic population, a broad category that includes people whose ancestral origins lie in the Iberian peninsula, Cuba, Puerto Rico, Mexico, and every country of South and Central America. In all its reporting, the bureau emphasizes that Hispanics "may be of any race"; the category derives from geographic, not racial origins. (Until 1970 it counted them all as white.) Partly because so many people confuse culture with race, and also perhaps because many multiculturalists are eager to proclaim an end to the white majority, this distinction is often ignored. When asked by the census to specify their race, some 90 percent of Hispanics choose "white"; small proportions choose "black," "American Indian," and (in the case of Asian-descended immigrants from Latin America) even "Asian." To make matters even more confusing, the Census Bureau's own studies show that Hispanics, like members of other groups, sometimes check off different racial or ethnic categories at different times.[16]

But many newspapers and magazines routinely count all Hispanics (11.5 percent of the population in 1999) as non-white. So did President Clinton when he declared, in a 1997 commencement speech in San Diego, "Within the next three years here in California, no single race or ethnic group will make up a majority of the state's population." In the case of ethnic groups, whether any single one will constitute a majority (or for that matter ever did) depends on what you mean by that phrase, but in terms of race, the Census Bureau still counts California as about two-thirds white. If against common sense and their own wishes you lump all Hispanics together and count them as non-white, the Census Bureau's national prediction for 2050 is that whites will constitute 52.8 percent and blacks 13.2 percent of the population, while Hispanics will rise to 24.3 percent.[17] Long before that date, Hispanics will become, as the news media are fond of proclaiming, the largest "minority group" in the country—one with so little in common, however, that its overall size may not mean very much socially or politically.

All these projections, of course, depend on ignoring intermarriage. Once you become aware of the Census Bureau's own figures on intermarriage, it becomes difficult to accept the conventional categories at face value. What counts as white, Asian, or Hispanic today is dubious enough; when you project it into a future where intermarriage will almost certainly be even more common, the whole concept of racial and ethnic identification looks silly. Given the history of discrimination against blacks throughout most of American history, one can understand why most

civil rights groups are adamant about preserving group solidarity and affirmative-action entitlements by counting as
black anyone with a discernible trace of African ancestry,
and to hell with ambiguities. Regardless of rationale, however, the whole exercise of racial labeling has itself become
an expression of the regressive forces that Bernard DeVoto
called Yesterday. It denies rather than reveals what is actually happening to the American population.

Looking at them from a statistical distance, one might
conclude that average Americans in 2050 will be a bit darker
than today's whites but more nearly uniform than today's
population taken as a whole. The race problems of the past
will be well on the way to solution because the very idea of
races, always dubious, cannot possibly survive the amount
of mixing that will have occurred by then. "America the
Beige" will be the new national anthem; the golf champion
Tiger Woods (Asian, black, white, American Indian) will become the ethnic norm. A new creation myth will replace the
old.

Desirable as this outcome would be, however, it probably will not happen so soon or so simply. Hispanics and
Asians are intermarrying rapidly with whites and no doubt
will continue to do so. But as Michael Lind correctly
pointed out in a *New York Times Magazine* article (August
16, 1998) with the provocative title "The Beige and the
Black," intermarriage between whites and blacks, though
rapidly increasing, remains much less frequent. The future
that Lind sees makes a considerably less appealing picture:
"Increasingly, whites, Asians and Hispanics are creating a
broad community from which black Americans may be ex-

cluded." The chief reason, he suspects, is anti-black prejudice, which many immigrants either bring from their countries of origin or pick up from their American neighbors.
According to Lind's theory, the melting pot continues to
boil down distinctions, but blacks are once again left out of
the recipe. The result sometime in the next century, Lind
thinks, is likely to be a white-Asian-Hispanic majority
whose members are hard to differentiate from one another,
and a still unassimilated minority of blacks.

How such an outcome would affect culture is hard to
say, apart from the obvious fact that the menu of post-
cultural choices would include an even wider selection of
Latin and Asian dishes. But one might just as well be skeptical of Lind's pessimism as of the more optimistic forecast
sketched earlier. Sooner or later, even the modest but increasing rate of intermarriage between black and other
Americans is bound to undermine what still stands of the
wall that has formally or informally segregated the descendants of Africans since shortly after Captain John Smith
sailed away from Jamestown. Although Lind points out that
many blacks frown on intermarriage (and he might have
added that organized black opposition since the early 1970s
has drastically reduced the number of interracial adop-
tions), there is no powerful principle of cultural exclusiveness in black America equivalent, for example, to that
among Orthodox Jews.

What good reason is there for doubting that the decline of racial bias visible over the past half-century will
continue? Except where law or prejudice forbids it, marriage is the most individual of choices. In a society of di-

verse origins and falling barriers, the results sooner or later drive believers in ethnic purity crazy. Why should anyone believe that an already mixed minority population whose palest members are described for anachronistic reasons as black will not become still paler and more ambiguous? On whatever schedule it happens, this process will contain the same familiar mixture of gain and loss as does the blurring of any other vivid, historic identity.

Some writers and moviemakers have long fantasized the total disappearance of visible African descent in a national orgy of miscegenation that finishes off America's race problems once and for all. "In a few thousand years," airily forecasts a white Canadian Harvard student in William Faulkner's 1936 novel *Absalom, Absalom!*, "I who regard you will also have sprung from the loins of African kings." The makers of the 1998 film *Bulworth* offered a similar vision. This eventuality may seem as far-fetched as the one Lind predicts. But what difference does it make? In the absence of complete ghettoization, the idea of irreconcilable black and white "cultures" is a mirage. Post-culturalism already includes black Americans. They have been gaining and losing from it in exactly the same ways as everyone else. The further it goes, the less systematic difference there will be for anyone to make a federal case of. Supremacists and separatists of any race, who feel threatened to the point of violence by the blending of old identities, will have lost their reason for being.

Yesterday is not coming back, either in the sometimes attractive guise of distinct ethnic cultures or in the uglier shape of racial hierarchy. Intermarriage of all kinds is both a cause and an irreversible consequence of the end of cultures. "Despite the census," the sociologist and communitarian writer Amitai Etzioni maintains, "America becomes more of a single community every day." He goes on to ask: "If the census allowed Americans to leave racial identity behind, is it unrealistic to imagine that many other institutions—colleges, businesses, courtrooms—might follow?" Of all the distinctions among people that post-cultural individualism blurs, race is the one that humanity could most profitably let go of. Etzioni is not the only prominent optimist. "The racial divide that has plagued America since its founding is fading fast," the Harvard sociologist Orlando Patterson prophesied at the beginning of 2000—"made obsolete by migratory, sociological, and biotechnological developments that are already under way. By the middle of the twenty-first century, America will have problems aplenty. But no racial problem whatsoever."[18] In 2050, if the Census Bureau still feels an atavistic need to keep statistics on race and ethnicity at all, one hopes it will finally provide a category for "Mixed," which more and more of the American population can happily check.

Chapter Four

Mass
Individualism and
the End of Culture

> *One's-Self I sing, a simple separate*
> *person,*
> *Yet utter the word Democratic, the word*
> *En-Masse,*

Walt Whitman proclaimed a few years after the Civil War.
As he so often did, the prolix poet laureate of democracy
stated the central American paradox more concisely than
anyone else. Although observers from Alexis de Tocqueville
and Ralph Waldo Emerson in the 1830s to a legion of cultural critics in the 1990s have scrutinized it from many an-
gles, no writer and no society have ever fully solved the
riddle of how individuals can remain individual in a large,
egalitarian democracy. The problem is not only one of lib-

erty, as Whitman himself had already discovered. Since his time, with the decline of cultural distinctions among groups and therefore among the individuals who comprise them, the difficulty of preserving individual differences has increased. Mass individualism, an individualism without much individuality, is one result.

Individualism is a word, like *multiculturalism*, that sets off firebells in the night. Although it originated as a liberal concept, liberals today often think of it as little more than a polite synonym for selfishness. Conservatives frequently use it as a synonym for entrepreneurship, as if economics were the only game in their town. Describing somebody as a rugged individualist (in modern usage there seems to be no other kind, any more than independence can avoid being fierce) summons up images of John Wayne beating the tar out of some city slicker from back East. When commentators here or abroad refer to the United States as an individualistic society, a label that goes back to de Tocqueville's *Democracy in America*, they rarely intend it as a compliment. What does individualism, the word or the thing, mean in the post-cultural age? Understanding some of its historical associations is a prerequisite to the necessarily more speculative and impressionistic task of grasping what contemporary America has made of it.

Individualism is not, when used properly, a synonym for selfishness or narcissism. Many selfish people are not individualists (on the contrary, they depend on others to an intolerable extent); many individualists are not selfish. Nor is it an antonym for community—individualists may be as gregarious and cooperative, even uncompetitive, as anyone else. Like multiculturalism or any other ideal that enjoins respect for an abstract other, individualism depends on universal and egalitarian assumptions—about the value and dignity of all cultures in the first case, about the equal rights and standing of all individuals in the second. The contrary of universalism is tribalism, the conviction that, as Ruth Benedict put it, outside one's own group there are no human beings. The opposite of individualism is collectivism, the belief that some larger body—the nation, the proletariat, the church, the white race, French culture—is more valuable or important than the individuals who make it up.

Conceptually, individualism is the assertion that individuals are the ultimate object of moral attention; that groups—families, tribes, nations, even species—have no more or other value than that of the individuals who make them up; and that those same individuals are entitled to act separately according to their own beliefs, wishes, or needs as long as they do not hinder other individuals following the same principle. Up to a point, individuals have not only a right but a responsibility to rely on their own judgments and efforts—though the precise placing of that point may be debated. The actions of any collective body (the government, "society," the PTA) are to be judged on the basis of how they affect the lives of actual human individuals, not just abstractions like the public interest.

The subjective identity of the individual, according to this view of life, is, or can be, or should be, distinguishable from and more important than his or her identity as a member of any collectivity. My being a specific me, your being a unique you, carries greater weight than our belonging to a particular ethnic group, sex, race, nationality. This recognition allows the possibility that individuals may, as the power of a culture over them declines, create momentary identities using bits and pieces from different groups as raw materials, reassembling them in unstable combinations. Individualism makes possible the Schandler-Wongs.

Individualism defined this way is not a political position and points in no predictable political direction. While it may nonetheless have political implications, as we shall see, those implications are rarely evident to people who in their individualism are simply going along with the crowd. Its emphasis on the self and low regard for the public world make it responsible for some of the limitations of contemporary democracy. In addition to a much-studied loss of civic-mindedness and decline in voting, the extraordinary inconsistency (sometimes called "volatility") of the American electorate since the 1960s suggests that in most voters' judgment the freedom to make private choices in most areas of life has little relation to political decisions. Much of the population seems to believe that the things it really cares about exist outside the political system, at least the part of the system that elections can touch, and therefore that elections are of comparatively minor importance. One telling example is that in contemporary usage the most common meaning of *choice* refers not to collective decisions such as voting but to the privacy-based right of abortion, the most important symbolic challenge to "traditional" morality and one that has proved virtually invulnerable to political reversal.

Because this kind of individualism is so closely identified with personal gratification and a repudiation of, even
contempt for, government, it can coexist on a casual basis
with many political points of view, as long as they make few
demands. The Victorian individualism of John Stuart Mill
or Lord Acton had at its center an austere emphasis on con-
science, but the kind of individualism we are talking about
here is far more oriented to pleasure—the desires of the
self, not its duties. The apparent shallowness and lack of
commitment that accompany it often drive the ideologically
engaged, left or right, to extremes of frustration. "In the
Red Army," Mao Tse-tung wrote in 1929, "there are also
quite a few people whose individualism finds expression in
pleasure-seeking. They always hope that their unit will
march into big cities. They want to go there not to work but
to enjoy themselves. The last thing they want is to work in
the Red areas where life is hard."[1] The rise of McWorld, as
we shall see in the next chapter, has made matters much
worse from this point of view.

Even a minimal individualism does, however, carry
with it the quasi-political implication that all persons have
rights encompassing more than superficial pleasure: life,
liberty, the pursuit of happiness. . . . Just because they are
human beings, they have claims that groups, governments,
and other individuals are bound to respect. Hence the
phrase "human rights." So long as we refrain from bothering anyone else, we are each at liberty to follow our own
pursuits, whatever they may be. Of course the question of
what constitutes bothering someone else is endlessly dis-
putable—shooting at them? playing your car radio too loud?

going to the supermarket naked?—but the principle is as clear as most principles. Correspondingly, individualism carries with it a suspicion not just of governments but of all powerful groups.

"Society," like government, is much more apt to be seen as a threat to freedom and integrity than as a support. Individuals are unique; "society" tries to crush anyone who gets out of line—this profoundly romantic view is held by virtually all American youth. To them it seems the most obvious common sense, despite the fact that "society," whether in the form of schools that have grown too large or parents who have grown too distant, is so much more indulgent of their wishes than it was half a century ago. The suspicion of social tyranny is not new; Emerson, long ago the national sage, declared in his most famous essay that "Society everywhere is in conspiracy against the manhood of every one of its members."[2] Since few people today read Emerson, the ubiquity of his views suggests that this version of individualism need not be a considered opinion arrived at through reflection, but can be breathed in like the air. One might even describe individualism as culturally induced if it were not in principle so at odds with the claims of culture to obedience.

In its recognizable modern forms, individualism began in the seventeenth century as European churches and monarchies began to break down. A century later, the doctrine that human rights derive self-evidently from the nature of human beings was most memorably enshrined in the Declaration of Independence. In its late twentieth-century version, the argument (often made today explicitly by libertarians but widely accepted semi-consciously by people who have not thought much about it) runs something like this: members of a modern society all have the demonstrable capacity to make different choices, follow different directions in life. People vary; even within the same culture they exhibit a myriad of different tastes and needs. In the absence of a universally persuasive religion or culture that dictates particular choices for everyone, no one is entitled to prevent our individually making such choices in whatever way we think will best advance our own happiness.

Although the Declaration of Independence drew on Nature's God as the granter of human rights, today the case for them is more often expressed in arguments independent of any religious basis. Even if no creator endowed us with anything—if we are the products of purely natural, Darwinian processes—we still possess those rights to life, liberty, and the pursuit of happiness simply because we are the sort of creatures we are. And besides, no one else has the right to take them away from us without good cause. There are limits to our freedom of choice, but only the limits necessary to protect other people's equal rights. For example, slavery is wrong regardless of what any given individual or culture thinks of it because it contradicts the entire set of egalitarian premises.[3]

The same kind of naturalistic argument that underlies the anthropological theory of powerful cultures can also support the liberation from culture and any other force that restricts individuals' freedom to pursue their own private ends. At least by implication, individualism insists that some rights trump cultural relativism (the slavery example), at least some of the time. Post-culturalism means weakened cultures; unless some other collective force such as the authoritarian state takes their place, it strengthens the role of individuals. Today, often shorn of its earlier attachment to laissez-faire economic views, individualism has become an instinct, even in precincts where the word itself is repudiated. Practically every American is an individualist. Mass individualism lies at the heart of post-culturalism, and vice versa.

The fact that the American political tradition places individual liberty ahead of almost every other goal has many benefits, not least of which is that it reduces occasions for intergroup conflict. The libertarian universalism that Gary Chapman described is one of the permanent trends in American life and comes closer to realization with every advance in communications. No wonder that authoritarian governments fear the Internet and try ineffectually to restrict it. Unfortunately the seemingly individualistic escape from restraint that the Internet symbolizes, at least in relatively free countries, may have less to do with an Enlightenment ideal of human fulfillment than with the narcissistic experience of one's own personality, now strengthened by its reflection in the computer screen, as the only significant reality.

Because the major constituents of cultures—kinship, religion, ethics, manners, rituals of all kinds, criteria for distinguishing between truth and falsehood—have been shrinking so rapidly as authorities over individual behavior, a major corollary to this kind of individualism is the "nonjudgmentalism" that Alan Wolfe described as the eleventh commandment, outweighing all others. Part of the visceral reluctance to judge other people's private conduct (as long as they embrace none of the anti-universalist taboos such as racism) is just an egalitarian lack of confidence—if I can judge you, you might someday judge me. But it also derives from a genuine, if poorly thought out, conviction that individuals are absolute sovereigns in their own lives.

But even monarchs need road maps. Once culture goes, what takes its place as millions of individuals who consider themselves free and independent try to chart their way through the minefields of life? One obvious answer is government, which plays a larger role than ever before in realms where culture used to legislate, such as child-rearing, education, relations between the sexes, the maintenance of ethnic identity, the ingredients that certain packaged foods must contain, the standards hairdressers have to meet in order to be licensed . . . the list of regulations in everyday life is nearly endless. But few individuals consider government a guide to living. What are the more spontaneous, unplanned substitutes for culture? There are many answers, some of which we have already seen, that at bottom add up to no answer.

Nostalgia. People claim an identity based on a narrow selection of their grandparents or great-grandparents; worse still, on the victimization of their grandparents. Whole armies of people suddenly dress up in Union or Confederate uniforms to reenact the battles of the Civil War. (This time Confederates outnumber Yankees because the South is Yesterday, and the whole point of this sad identity game is that the past wins.) Or the sudden passion since the 1970s for genealogy—the projection of the self into the past, the elimination of everything in the past that did not lead directly to the self—which becomes for many people the only interesting kind of history. Or for some intellectuals, as we saw in Chapter 2, multiculturalism itself takes the place of a lost culture, just as religiosity, the belief that religion in general is a good thing, so often takes the place of a lost faith.

Entertainment. But to a far greater extent, especially for the young, entertainers take the place of culture: singers and movie stars who communicate values of a sort to live by. How many people young or old take contemporary leaders (let alone past heroes who represent self-sacrifice) as seriously as they take rock singers and movie stars? Like it or not, the music video is the major international art form of our time. The influence of entertainment on behavior has, of course, been studied obsessively since the rise of television in the 1950s. There is still no consensus as to whether watching violence on the screen contributes to violence in real life, particularly among children and teenagers; the strongest impact anyone can identify with certainty is on clothing styles and speech habits. For our purposes here, the salient point is that entertainers, simply by being the focus of such attention, popularize what was already the conventional wisdom and extend its applications ever further in the minds of their fans: do what you want, as aggressively as you want; no one has the right to tell you what to do, what not to do, how to do it, when or where to do it, who to do it with. Whatever does not come from within you is an imposition. Since one of the most important traditional functions of culture is to control male tendencies toward aggression and polygyny, its decline makes these biologically coded forms of behavior more visible on the screen and in real life.

Personality. At the collective level, bureaucracy expands to fill the vacuum of culture. But personality, encouraged at every step by television and theme parks, film and tape, music and malls, fills it at the private level. Each of these realms imitates the other, competing with it: bureaucratic jargon in private life ("family management," "negotiating" with one's children); first names (often nicknames) everywhere in public. The power of entertainers always brings us back to personality, to the individual who is not merely self-defined and self-reliant but self-enclosed. Your personality, they promise, is the most important thing in the world. Again Emerson was there before us: "To believe your own thought, to believe that what is true for you in your private heart is true for all men,—that is genius." "The whole theory of the universe," Whitman added a few years later, "is directed unerringly to one single individual—namely to You."[4] If your temperament is too shy or inhibited to act on such a belief, or if grief for a loved one depresses you with its reminder of the universal fate, an avalanche of new mood-altering pills and therapies can quickly solve the problem.

One consequence of all these developments is the radical subjectivism of American popular and academic "culture" today. This subjectivism is not only the natural consequence of the primacy of the self—what difference could an external fact or rule make?—but also a way of avoiding conflict, judgmentalism, suggestions that we might not all be equal. If every self occupies the same level, why should their beliefs not be treated as equally true too? To say otherwise is at least implicitly to accuse some people of being wrong, perhaps even stupid. Post-cultural selves are often fragile creations (another reason for all those new pills), prone to view themselves as victims of prejudice or abuse. How much safer and more comfortable, when disagreement is unavoidable, to say that you have your way, I have my way. Whether the matter under consideration has to do with factual accuracy or morality, everything becomes a matter of individual taste or "lifestyle," therefore immune to censure. Somewhat the same premise lay behind one of the most popular TV game shows of all time, "Family Feud," where the goal was to guess not the correct or most reasonable answer to a question but the response given most often by other Americans in a poll. Thus the translation of equality and democracy to the cognitive realm.

College students express a variant of the same subjectivism when they announce, as if it were self-evident, that everyone—*everyone*—has different beliefs about religion, government, marriage, ethics, beauty . . . whatever. When it comes to behavior, contrary to the intentions of the anthropologists who gave it currency, cultural relativism in American life has evolved to the point where the particular claims of all cultures are simply ignored whenever they become peremptory. Western monogamy and traditional Muslim polygamy are morally equivalent to many Americans who would be surprised to hear themselves described as multi-

culturalists. Their sympathy for other cultures is not necessarily greater than that of previous generations, but almost
all cultural limitations on individual behavior have come to
seem equally outdated, arbitrary, and meaningless. The ancient stigma against having children out of wedlock has
nearly disappeared for the same reason. Why get married at
all if you think some other lifestyle would suit you better?

The unpopularity of the so-called religious right, not
only with liberal intellectuals but with many people who are
neither liberal nor intellectual, rests on the suspicion that it
represents a return to a judgmental, exclusive notion of culture that most Americans have no wish to revisit. A polite
relativism that began centuries ago with religion, where differences are impossible to settle with convincing proof, has
spread gradually to all matters of judgment, and often to
matters of fact as well. This distrust of certainty cuts in both
directions, however. To the consternation of biologists, polls
indicate that a large majority would allow creationism equal
time in the biology classroom with evolution—not necessarily, as in earlier times, because of strong religious convictions, but in the interests of tolerance and the equality of
opinions.

As noted earlier, attacks on the objectivity of science
are a major feature of cultural studies programs in universities today. They occupy a corner of the academy where traditional religion is particularly unfashionable. Unlike these
academic attitudes, the main source of popular subjectivism was not, as Allan Bloom and other Jeremiahs have
sometimes complained, average Americans' gullibility toward the recondite philosophers of Weimar Germany or

their French deconstructionist descendants. Its real foun-
tainhead was the homegrown American belief in equality,
which easily led to a distrust of intellectuals and intellectual exertion of any kind that might cause dissension. In a
society with such diverse opinions, defining all beliefs as
equally matters of faith makes life easier. Purely technical
thinking, with less potential for raising offense, is an exception, particularly if it has an obvious practical application.

At its worst, this subjectivism amounts to the obscure
conviction that nothing is good or true unless it satisfies me
at this moment. It carries the doctrine that goodness and
truth are culturally relative to what is in a sense its logical
final step, individual relativism. Not only are cultures immune to outside criticism, but so are groups and individuals, because criticism of their behavior constitutes a
forbidden instance of "imposing your values on others."
Whether those values are religious, scientific, or neither
makes little difference. Once again, the roots of the attitude
are a hybrid of American popular philosophy and assimilated anthropology. Emerson the transcendental subjectivist
dared his readers to believe: "Good and bad are but names
very readily transferable to that or this; the only right is
what is after my constitution, the only wrong what is
against it. . . . We denote this primary wisdom as Intuition,
whilst all later teachings are tuitions."[5]*

---

*A paradoxical effect of this subjective individualism is to cast suspicion
on traditional doctrines of free speech, since speech can so easily disturb
or suggest that someone is morally or factually in the wrong. In *Schenck
v. United States*, Justice Oliver Wendell Holmes wrote: "The most strin-
gent protection of free speech would not protect a man in falsely shout-

The French philosopher Pierre Manent recently expressed an unintended consequence of this kind of subjectivism, including a paradoxical loss of conviction in one's
own subjectivity:

> Seeking his own good, the modern man of human
> rights will feel intensely that no one has a right to keep
> him from it. But simultaneously he will agree that he
> has no right to constrain his neighbor in the name of
> the good—that is, that the good he seeks has no claim
> on his neighbor because the constraint of others, even
> for the good, leads to the greatest of evils, war. But if
> my good cannot become law for my neighbor, can it be
> a very serious law for me? Why would I not abandon,
> or at least treat lightly, something that my neighbor has
> the right to do without? . . . And every person's right to
> seek his good eventually becomes the right not to seek
> the good at all.[6]

Everything becomes a matter of taste because an objective
standard of right and wrong, better or worse, leads unavoidably to conflict and someone's potential loss of self-esteem.
As a result, the same open-mindedness that advances harmonious relations among people of so many different back-

ing fire in a theater and causing a panic." This celebrated opinion is constantly quoted by journalists and politicians as stating a self-evident limit
to free speech, nearly always with "falsely" left out. To those who quote it
in this inaccurate form, the question of whether the theater is actually
burning appears to have no relevance. The members of an audience, or
whatever group in society it symbolizes, have a right not to be upset no
matter what their objective peril.

grounds undermines conviction in the very differences it was intended to accommodate. The word *absolute* becomes a term of contemptuous dismissal in discussions of values or facts, a word that ends all arguments. The stresses and strains, the sheer unnaturalness, of maintaining this perpetual neutrality lead in turn to explosions of the self-contradictory censoriousness that Michael Polanyi called moral inversion.

For not *everything* anyone wants to do privately is a matter of unfettered choice. In any society, some activities are freer than others. Sometimes the basis for distinguishing between the permitted and the forbidden would be hard for an outsider to understand. Nor is it always a matter of majority tastes defining what a minority are free to do, as opponents of the war on drugs often charge. In the United States today, the stigma attached to active homosexuality is less, at least among the intelligentsia, than that attached to smoking, though far more people smoke than are homosexual. (The two are not mutually exclusive.) Laws proliferate against tobacco and its users even as the remaining laws that criminalize homosexual practices are being repealed or forgotten. Until the 1970s exactly the reverse was true: homosexual activity was often illegal and nearly always disapproved of, while smoking, though its dangers had been widely publicized for twenty years, was accepted almost everywhere.

As the decline in anti-homosexual feeling is one of the great triumphs of the general rule of libertarian non-judgmentalism in private behavior, so the crusade against tobacco and its users is probably the largest-scale exception to that rule in present-day America. There seems to be little logic to this selective and shifting puritanism, except perhaps the opposed rule that a safety valve, a licensed exception to the eleventh commandment, is always necessary to accommodate an irresistible human urge to disapprove. Moral inversion is not only a characteristic of intellectuals. The urge to define some activity as a major national threat becomes all the more desperate in a period of overweening tolerance. Proportionately to the strength of this suppressed passion, the target of prohibition must be a common indulgence, and it may change for no predictable reason—from alcohol in the early twentieth century to comic books (supposedly the root of juvenile delinquency) in the 1950s to tobacco at the century's end.

If truth and goodness can be found only within the self, and are wholly relative to its unique needs, of what value are education and experience, parental wisdom or cultural tradition? Rationality, restraint, and deferred gratification are out. Adolescent, highly emotional styles of expression are in. As in Romantic poetry, being a child or a youth is better in every way than being an adult. Although children are the object of tremendous sentiment and the stated justification for nearly every new political proposal, adolescence is the age group most widely imitated. People of both sexes and every age dress in jeans and sneakers and T-shirts; nearly everyone over thirty in every walk of life tries to seem younger, to demonstrate youthful tastes and attitudes.

"Young" is a compliment at any chronological stage. "Mature" in most contexts means over the hill. "Adult language" means profanity; an adult community is a retirement home. Finding one's way back to the inner child is an approved goal, but few authorities suggest that children should search for an inner grown-up. No wonder contemporary American attempts at nonconformity so often center on personal appearance rather than on qualities that require a more developed character. In other countries where American influence on culture has penetrated, what first strikes most observers is the impact of the same American youth styles of dress and entertainment—jeans and baseball caps, Nikes and rock music, slang from imported movies or television, Marlboro cigarettes.

The adulation of youth at home or abroad is another aspect of the revolt against culture, which values the experience and authority of age, the knowledge of older or wider things than one's self. Forget about otherness; to the youth-oriented individualist, all the world's a mirror, an invitation to self-exhibition. A foreign culture, a literary work from a previous century, an event from the past holds no interest unless updated, all its confusing differentness removed, remade into an expression of contemporary concerns, contemporary emotions (basic ones that everyone can share), a flatterer of me, now. Walt Disney makes Pocahontas a multicultural cartoon role model for the nineties by transforming her into a slim, sexy, caring eco-feminist. A new Disney theme park in central Virginia would have made all of American history equally user-friendly to people whose only interest is in costumed versions of themselves—if a coalition of environmentalists and historians had not protested so loudly that the project was canceled. A few miles up the road from Jamestown, Colonial Williamsburg has turned the eighteenth century into a popular line of housewares. "The First Amendment," proclaims Michael Eisner, chairman of the Walt Disney Company, "gives you the right to be plastic." Who really wants to know more about the Kurds or the Crusades?

Despite the worldwide ascendancy of American youth culture, the incarnation of post-cultural individualism at the end of the twentieth century was not an American at all. When the young Lady Diana Spencer married Charles, Prince of Wales, in 1981, she immediately became a fairy-tale princess whose picture (usually, at that stage, with her husband) adorned every popular magazine and whose hairstyle quickly became the most celebrated fashion of the decade. As all the world knows, it was not a happy marriage. Chosen for her blood line, her virginity, her looks, her healthy capacity to bear heirs, and her presumed docility, Diana soon began to rebel against the anachronisms of Buckingham Palace life. Even a semi-arranged marriage deeply offends individualism, and Diana began to feel like a victim of a dying institution's archaic needs. Unlike earlier generations of high-profile royals, the princess was not prepared to suffer in silence the demands of protocol, the impersonal formality that constitutional tradition imposes on the royal family, or the infidelity of her husband. When her marriage began to come apart, she sought maximum public attention.

Needless to say, the whole situation was ideal material

for tabloid journalism, which in its operatic cultivation of emotionally exaggerated, intensely dramatized situations constantly strives for myth and archetype. After her death, Diana's brother, the current Lord Spencer, bitterly accused the press of having hounded her to her death, but matters were considerably more complicated. Nearly everyone recognized that Diana had used the press as much as it had used her. She had from the start been a natural object for their attentions, but beginning at the time she separated from Charles she had recast herself as the most elegant (and in many ways the most cooperative) emblem in history for their perennial concerns.

Instead of concealing her feelings and personality behind a veil of royal privacy, she revealed everything—at least everything she wanted to reveal. She gave a famous television interview in which she bared her emotions toward the institutions she felt were trying to suppress her personality and desires. She posed for the cover of *Vanity Fair*. She became a practiced leaker of information to the media, information that naturally made her look good and the rest of the royal family, particularly her unglamorous husband and the queen, seem cold and unfeeling. From the standpoint of the monarchy, whose survival in a democratic age depends on the very suppression of personality and emotions that Diana complained of, she became a royal nuisance.

Above all, she presented herself as a free-spirited woman of the future who had become a victim of the past. What, after all, was the most cherished kind of freedom on the eve of the millennium? Not freedom of speech, which can so easily conflict with the command to avoid offense or judgment. Free speech is always dangerous because of its potential for disturbance. We have already seen that the disagreements it articulates call into question the equality of opinions and information, and therefore of those who hold them. From an egalitarian point of view, sexual freedom is much safer, more congruent with the idealization of youth, capable of making everyone feel sophisticated merely by endorsing it—the one freedom that nobody, certainly no popular journalist or politician, dares argue with today on pain of being denounced as a hypocrite, a religious bigot, or worst of all a survivor from the 1950s. Princess Diana had lovers, publicly, openly, on the front pages of the tabloids. She talked openly about her personal desires. Her last lover, whom she was hoping to marry when they died together on a street in Paris, the city of love, was an Arab, a Muslim, a man widely described as being of another race. Once again she had transgressed the discredited demands of a dying culture.

Through a whole series of actions, some of them spontaneous, others shrewdly planned, Diana transformed herself into a different kind of princess for the post-cultural age, combining freedom and nostalgia in an unsurpassable blend. Nostalgia for a glamorous, idealized past of royal princes and princesses—the essence of fairy tale. Freedom to live one's own life with no inhibitions, to love a succession of handsome men or beautiful women in a world of palaces, yachts, and five-star hotels. If part of the audience felt guilty projecting such fantasies onto a woman who had been born to luxury and never had to do without it, they could always be reminded of the charities she worked for—popular causes such as AIDS, children, land mines, Africa.

Wherever a barrier seemed to block her path, she was photographed crossing it. No one else could have summed up in a short, unhappy life so many of the themes of post-cultural yearning. Her death at thirty-six transformed her into a martyr to faceless institutions, the royal rebel whose fate at last raised tabloid to the status of universal myth and scripture, the object of a worldwide cult—a Pocahontas in reverse for the end of the millennium.

Culture, including manners, morals, and law, was an impersonal set of patterns to which everyone who belonged was subject. Informality signals a loss of belief in whatever aspect of culture is being bypassed, a substitution of personality for tradition. The decline of parents' and teachers' authority over children has critically weakened the transmission of culture from one generation to the next, as well as the more formal values of adulthood. After cultures, the private and personal become more important to most people than any impersonal substitute for culture. They are both a sign of the self's victory over its oppressors and a refuge from a vast, intimidating public world empty of any content that connects with how they see their lives or what they would like to be. The impact of these changes on public life is no less significant than their effects on private lives.

"By the 1970s," writes the historian Alonzo L. Hamby, "it had become a handicap for an aspirant to the presidency to have a close affiliation with a political establishment or to have any sort of strongly defined ethnic, religious, or regional identity. Such characteristics only diminished one's image from the perspective of a homogeneous, independent electorate."[7] What "independent" means in this context is the kind of apolitical individualism associated with post-culturalism, where people vote for their impression of a personality rather than a party. (A personality in this sense is not the same thing as a character, let alone a history.) This inflation of personality at the expense of external reality did not begin with the computer age, nor even with Emerson. The late historian Christopher Lasch chronicled its gradual rise in a 1978 book entitled (naturally) *The Culture of Narcissism*. Computers and their sibling cable television have, however, greatly accelerated the process in politics as elsewhere.

Both liberal and conservative politicians concluded long ago that voters are more interested in personal warmth as communicated by television than in ideological positions. The favorite political event is now the so-called town meeting, a carefully staged opportunity to display that warmth, whose name conveys nostalgia for an older, more intimate self-governing community. For the same reasons, candidates whose first names have more than one syllable routinely run under boyish nicknames, a custom that began in the South and conquered the rest of the country around the end of the eighties. Virtually the only time President Clinton's full name was ever used in public after he started running for office in the 1970s was during his impeachment and trial, when his opponents spat out the full seven sylla- bles, *William Jefferson Clinton*, as if to say that by his crimes he had forfeited the right to be known as Bill. This complex of changes is exactly what one would expect in the transition to post-culturalism. For a politician to resist it is to risk being seen as cold and elitist. Whatever idealistic ob- servers may have thought about it all, contenders for elec- tive office either caught on or soon found themselves retired. The cultural assumptions that allowed Franklin Roosevelt and even Ronald Reagan a degree of dignity and distance have simply evaporated.

So has, at least in good times, most of the impersonal attraction of specific ideas about governing. To be driven by political conviction nowadays is to be partisan; to be parti- san is one more way of being judgmental and threatening. The proportion of voters who describe themselves as loyal to a particular party has been declining steadily for more than three decades. "Bipartisanship," or "non-partisanship," may be a self-contradictory ideal for political competition in a democracy, but its popularity today perfectly mirrors the nostalgic, non-judgmental attitudes we have been talking about. The only way to preserve the fiction of universal in- clusiveness in a post-cultural election campaign is to make it a referendum on the personality of someone familiar and ordinary enough to be known by his nickname, with the candidate's children thrown in as props. Like the idea of a town meeting, the political display of parenthood suggests comfortingly that regardless of whatever strife may be occurring in the nation or the world, in its heart America is still an old-fashioned family.

The news media too have gone farther in the direction of post-cultural informality and subjectivism than most of their own professionals would have believed possible even ten years ago. The endlessly televised scenes of hugging and weeping that now symbolize any national trauma, from a lost football game to mass murder in a school, capture the decline of ritual and the formlessness of what takes its place among participants and media alike. Tabloidism—the abandonment of traditional moral reticence in news coverage, of respect for privacy, of an impersonal concern with fact, in favor of a total emphasis on personality, sexual behavior, and emotions for their own sake—is now a permanent part of ABC News and the *New York Times*, to say nothing of the less elite media, and not only as a legacy of the Clinton experience. In the information age, with more sources of knowledge available than ever before, the public's general level of information about its national life is probably as low as it has ever been.[8]

Although they agonized about it from time to time, the quality end of the news business gradually went along with the tabloids because they knew that most of their audience, deep down, was more interested in the personal lives of public figures than in anything else about them—demonstrably more curious about their sex lives than their policies or politics. The fact that for eight years Clinton survived such an avalanche of lavishly reported scandals can be explained by many factors, not all of which have anything to do with post-culturalism. But the effectiveness of his appeal to personal charm, to his attractive family, and above all to the emotionally fluent, non-judgmental inclusiveness so central to post-cultural life shows that he understood the Zeitgeist better than his adversaries did.

"To believe that what is true for you in your private heart is true for all men,—that is genius." "The only right is what is after my constitution." By presenting himself in the Monica Lewinsky controversy as a courageous, warm-hearted victim under assault for violating the sexual taboos of an extinct culture, the most powerful man in the world made himself the symbol of a long-familiar American ideal that had finally been made flesh at the highest level. No wonder so much of the public supported him against adversaries who had been successfully typed as repressed, puritanical partisans. Adultery, H. L. Mencken once wrote, is the application of democracy to love.[9] Like Princess Diana, like a celebrity in a clever advertisement, like the hero of Jack Kerouac's prophetic novel *On the Road* who made love unscathed to a different woman at every stop on his endless journey, Clinton embodied some of their deepest wishes.

Many more people read or watch commercial advertisements than political news, and advertising has always been filled with famous people (rarely politicians) who seem to promise that you can be just like them if you buy the product they happen to be advertising. Now, paradoxically, buying the product will also make you more of an individual, more yourself. "Express yourself in a new Safari van from GMC," ran a much imitated ad of the 1980s. "Its personality is your personality!" Rarely are these promises designed to appeal to particular ethnic identities, though such identities are often present as marketing tools to reach an ethnically indistinct public of a particular age and income. Italian lovers advertise suits and shoes; Irish lovers advertise soap; French lovers advertise perfume. Always there is that double promise of wish fulfillment, the suggestion that the product will make you uniquely yourself as well as like the successful lovers in the picture.

An unreflective, ungrounded individualism organized around products flaunted by celebrities—the right clothes, the right car, the right electronics, the right fast food, the right enjoyments—has become the most visible attitude toward life in America at the turn of the millennium. To say the least, it is an ironic kind of individualism in which a great many people without much confidence search television, the shopping malls, the literature of self-help, the Internet until they find a mass-produced simulacrum of their own identity, and as a result end up seeming very much alike. ("The first thing that strikes the eye," de Tocqueville wrote scornfully in the 1830s, "is an innumerable multitude of men, all equal and alike, incessantly endeavoring to procure the petty and paltry pleasures with which they glut their lives."[10] Once more, no social development is entirely new.) These are the insecure selves for whose reaffirmation talk radio and call-in television were invented. At a higher level of literacy, the same insecurity about identity has turned the confessional memoir into a flourishing, depressingly formulaic literary genre.

Half a century ago, when Max Lerner was writing *America as a Civilization*, a legion of best-selling commentators denounced conformity as the major curse of American life. The 1950s were rife with book titles such as William Whyte's *The Organization Man* and David Riesman's *The Lonely Crowd*. "The real dangers of the American mode of life," wrote Lerner, "are not in the machine or even in standardization as much as they are in conformism. . . . They flow rather from the mimesis of the dominant and successful by the weak and mediocre, from the intolerance of diversity, and from the fear of being thought different from one's fellows. This is the essence of conformism."[11]

By the 1980s the target had moved 180 degrees, with critics attacking what they now saw as the excessive individualism of the "Me" decade. Communitarianism by one name or another became the newest ideal of social thinkers. But life is more continuous than critics often recognize in the heat of the moment. The images of Thoreau at Walden Pond and Babbitt at the corporation are about equally engraved in the American psyche. In spite of de Tocqueville's warnings, few cultural commentators spotted the evolution of a conformist individualism rooted in the personalities of a population who had increasingly been reared on the same experiences, often felt most at home in the mechanical, rule-driven world of computers, and accepted without much questioning the same notions of what it meant to be free to satisfy one's desires.

Again, the doctrine of individualism is not the same

thing as the fact of individuality. One of the many paradoxes about post-culturalism is that it both increases and reduces the differences between one actual human being and another in the same society. As long as immigrant cultures remained powerful in American life, they often constricted their own members, but at the same time they kept them distinct from members of other cultures. While Irish-American Catholics might seem regimented to hostile observers, as a body they were impossible to confuse with WASPs, or even with Polish-American Catholics. Their worst enemies would not have described any of these groups as plastic. The decline of such differences in the twentieth century reduced both the constraints and the variety. A stable hierarchy of social class might have preserved an alternative source of differentiation, but the ideal of social mobility and the fact that such a large majority of Americans consider themselves middle class made class a much less important distinction in individuals' self-definition than it was in Europe.

John Stuart Mill's *On Liberty*, first published in 1859, remains the most important scripture of liberal individualism because Mill, a thinker whom Walt Whitman admired, so acutely analyzed problems that seem to have grown worse since his time. Most of all, formulating Whitman's paradox of a few years later in a philosophical idiom, he concerned himself with the problem of how individuals in a modern democracy can avoid being swallowed up by what, echoing de Tocqueville, he called "the tyranny of the majority."

For Mill as for Emerson and Whitman, the chief

enemy of individuality was custom, tradition, culture. He was one of the first writers to use the term "public opinion" for the form these nebulous entities take in a modern democracy. By any name, he was against it. "It is desirable," he began in his rather pedantic style, "that in things which do not primarily concern others, individuality should assert itself. Where, not the person's own character, but the traditions or customs of other people are the rule of conduct, there is wanting one of the principal ingredients of human happiness, and quite the chief ingredient of individual and social progress."[12] Spontaneity and eccentricity are important virtues in Mill's writings, not just for the individual who practices them but for innovation in society as a whole.

To be sure, the collective experience of the human race is also valuable; no one ever starts from zero. Mill was not recommending the Wordsworthian theory of the child as the "best philosopher," who appears in the world prepackaged with all useful knowledge in its newborn self. "But," he complained, "society has now fairly got the better of individuality; and the danger which threatens human nature is not the excess, but the deficiency, of personal impulses and preferences." During a period of material progress and rising democracy, this threat was growing ever worse: "In our times, from the highest class of society down to the lowest, everyone lives as under the eye of a hostile and dreaded censorship."[13] That censorship came not from priests, kings, or other traditional authorities but from the majority—the mass of average people imposing their tastes and practices on one another. Public opinion polling had not been invented in Mill's time, but he anticipated the sacred place it would occupy a century and a half later. For the implicit premise of polling, as of democracy in its crudest formulation, is that all opinions are equal and only numbers count.

Although Mill strongly believed in democracy, he feared it could easily reduce everyone and everything to the same level of indistinguishable mediocrity. So great an emphasis on equality encouraged a deadening sameness. In pre-democratic ages, he maintained, "the individual was a power in himself"; an individual with great talent or high social position could become a great power. No longer: "At present individuals are lost in the crowd." For the crowd as a crowd, the mass as a mass, Mill had nothing but contempt:

> Comparatively speaking, they now read the same things, listen to the same things, see the same things, go to the same places, have their hopes and fears directed to the same objects, have the same rights and liberties, and the same means of asserting them. Great as are the differences of position which remain, they are nothing to those which have ceased.[14]

In these prophetic sentences we can see ourselves. The problem today, Mill would agree, is not only the conformism implicit in democracy—the voice of the people is the voice of God, therefore each one should think and live as everyone else does—still less the residual force of custom, tradition, culture. It is also that after democracy and individual rights have helped to discredit those archaic forces, one of the inevitable (even if unforeseen) results is a mass individualism that encourages people to assert themselves in nearly identical ways.

Whether we focus on the sexual revolution, changing hairstyles, the popularity of baseball caps worn backward in restaurants, the fashion for genealogy, or the forms in which people express themselves on the Internet, the means that Americans choose for asserting their individuality are often anything but individual. "There is no reason," Mill insisted plaintively, "that all human existence should be constructed on some one or some small number of patterns."[15] He might now feel that while more lip service is paid today than in his era to nonconformity—expressing oneself, the individual against society, self-assertiveness, doing your own thing, creating your own lifestyle—there is at the same time a huge amount of self-deception about the nature of these rebellions against impotent customs.

Consider the example of an institution that directly affects about half of all Americans at an impressionable age and is often regarded as a haven for dissent, even activism: the university. In the humanities, the field I know best, opaque slogans about subverting the hegemonic white male logocentrism of Western culture and celebrating marginalized post-colonial otherness are the stuff of hundreds of books and thousands of lectures, hardly more than an institutional convention. The increased racial variety of faculties and student bodies over the past generation, an excellent thing in itself, obscures the sad fact that minority professors are so often expected to play an "oppositional" role whose rules and limits are rigidly specified. Despite the omnipresent rhetoric of political activism, few faculty members really practice it from any ideological direction. Those they teach are not much different, either in the sense of having deeper social commitments or of leading less conformist lives in other respects. Northern students who went south in 1964 to register black voters were performing a lonely, dangerous act that helped lead the country to a better future. Their much more numerous successors, who feel the thrill of virtue while singing "We Shall Overcome" at campus Martin Luther King Day ceremonies, are only sentimental voices in the crowd, a chorus echoing the safest conventional wisdom at an institutional occasion where sympathy for the oppressed merges seamlessly with public relations.

In America, because we began in revolution and have such a long history of expressing idealism in nonconformist terms, the most powerful orthodoxies frequently present themselves as heresies: a brave few rebels once again standing up to society. But when the embattled individual finally becomes, in the abstract, one of society's least controversial ideals—when the whole conception of countercultural values has lost its meaning—how can anyone manage to avoid conformity and be a real individual? Mill never envisioned such a *koan*-like reversal.

Nevertheless.

Shallow as these samples too often are, mass individualism still beats the alternative of overpowering collective identities that begin at birth or early in life. Where individuals are free, Mill would point out, they may act at their laziest or most foolish, they may be self-deceiving conformists, but the future remains open. If you really believe in human equality, you must accept people doing what *they* want to do, living the way that suits *them*, just as they are, instead of waiting until intellectuals or ideologues have finally taught them what they *should* want to do, have, and be. If that means they seem uncomfortably alike, spend a lot of time at the mall, never read a book, prefer rap to Mozart—or, if they happen to be intellectuals themselves, prefer Mahler because their own peer group prescribes him this year—well, so be it. The only alternative is a greater or lesser degree of authoritarianism that has no chance of success anyway, if success is defined as improving the taste and morals of the public according to a particular model. All anyone has a right to demand of other adults in the abstract is that they live up to their individual responsibilities and not interfere with the freedom or well-being of anyone else. The confusion of direction that results in American lives when the dictates of culture atrophy is a universal fact that no amount of exhortation or legislation is likely to change.

Moreover, not every average citizen will spend his days at Wal-Mart (a business that in any case sells useful merchandise at low prices), any more than every academic buys her opinions in bulk from National Public Radio. Stereotypes of all kinds have their limits, and even post-cultural mass individualism makes a deeper individuality a little more likely, in the same way that a relatively open mass market has led to an unimaginable variety of consumer products. "The impulse for liberty," Natalie Angier wrote half enthusiastically in the *New York Times Magazine* (February 21, 1999), "is congenital. It is the ultimate manifestation of selfishness, which is why we can count on its endurance."

Individual liberty, the nagging possibility of variety, does observably breed some actual variety, and keeps open to members of each generation the goal of real diversity in ways of thinking and living, as distinct from the bogus diversity of ancestor worship. Newborn babies are not Xeroxes of a single prototype; they vary from birth and if given sufficient chance will diverge increasingly as they mature. The more freedom people have, the more of them press the limits of whatever norms their society takes for granted. Look again at what the civil rights movement accomplished beginning in a decade notorious for conformity. Mass individualism deserves the two cheers that E. M. Forster conceded to democracy. Even on talk radio and Internet bulletin boards, not all the opinions expressed are thoughtless or ignorant.

The tangible benefits of mass individual freedom are sometimes less than obvious to idealists who write or read books like this one. Jack Donnelly makes a point often forgotten in all the *fin de siècle* claims of politicians and public intellectuals about rootless individualism, social atomization, an excessive emphasis on rights, and the need to strengthen communities, cultures, and tribes of one kind or another:

> For all the talk of excessive individualism, the problem in the world today is not too many individual rights but

that individual human rights are not sufficiently re-spected. States and societies have a variety of claims on individuals, and modern states have awesome pow-ers to bring individuals to their knees—if necessary, to break their minds as well as their bodies. Human rights, and parallel legal rights, are among the few re-sources of individuals in the face of the modern state. The balance is already (always?) tilted against the indi-vidual. . . .

Every day we see individuals crushed by society. Rarely, if ever, do we see society torn apart by the exer-cise of individual human rights. Social disorder and decay are instead usually associated with the *violation* of individual human rights by the state or some other organized segment of society.[16]

Throughout the 1990s some of the worst violations came from governments that claimed to represent not citi-zens but cultures, enforcing on individuals demands that al-lowed no appeal because their culture was larger than they were. One of the ironies of multiculturalism at the turn of the millennium is that the notion of human rights, origi-nally formulated to protect individuals against govern-ments, societies, and other threats to their autonomy and well-being, has been claimed by UNESCO as belonging to cultures themselves, which thereby acquire their own "right" to enforce conformity on rebellious individuals.[17] "There are fundamental freedoms to fight for," comments Salman Rushdie, the Indian-born British novelist sen-tenced to death by Iran for allegedly insulting Islam, in a

New York Times op-ed piece (March 5, 1999), "and it will not do to doom the terrorized women of Afghanistan or of the circumcision-happy lands of Africa by calling their oppression their 'culture.'" Continuing oppression in the name of culture and the doctrine of "cultural rights" remind us that while threats to individualism may seem small in the United States at present, people in many parts of the world have very different stories to tell.

Chapter Five

Toward a Post-
Cultural World?

In its basic assumptions, modern multiculturalism bears a striking resemblance to Isaiah Berlin's description of nationalism:

> ... the conviction, in the first place, that men belong to a particular human group, and that the way of life of the group differs from that of others; that the characters of the individuals who compose the group are shaped by, and cannot be understood apart from, those of the group, defined in terms of common territory, customs, laws, memories, beliefs, language, artistic and religious expression, social institutions, ways of life, to which some add heredity, kinship, racial charac-

teristics; and that it is these factors which shape human beings, their purposes and their values.

Secondly, that the pattern of life of a society is similar to that of a biological organism. . . . Whence it follows that the essential human unit in which man's nature is fully realised is not the individual, or a voluntary association which can be dissolved or altered or abandoned at will, but the nation . . .[1]

As this extended definition makes clear, the hierarchies of influence and the organic metaphors embodied in multiculturalism have their deepest roots in the romantic nationalism of the nineteenth century.

This relationship should remind us, if we really needed reminding, that culture is still a life-and-death issue in many parts of the world. North America, where civil wars and large-scale ethnic bloodshed have become nearly unimaginable, is far from the whole story. The time has come to cast a final look at where we have been and to see how much, or how little, the rest of the world resembles the American landscapes we have been surveying.

As noted earlier, multiculturalism began life in the early 1970s as a policy to placate groups who felt slighted by the Canadian government's official emphasis on biculturalism. The whole concept originated in the political needs of a country whose organization, if not its culture, is very different from that of the United States. Once launched, however, the ship—it is irresistible at times to think of multiculturalism as a modern replica of Noah's Ark—proved to have more sail than rudder and scudded unsteer-

ably before a succession of powerful winds. First one nationality group, then another, then groups that were not
ethnic (women, "sexual minorities," the handicapped) demanded passage. By the initial logic, they could not be refused tickets. The model rapidly altered to resemble an
old-fashioned big-city machine: something for the Irish,
something for the Italians, something for the Jews. . . .
From the start there was the explicit promise that law and
public money would intervene to save ethnic identities
(Ukrainian, Inuit, Hispanic) that were on the verge of dying
out in the open spaces of North America. Nostalgia was
present at the creation: multiculturalism as a government
policy to resist the effects of post-culturalism.

Multiculturalism was from the start a program and an
ideology. Its political implications follow naturally from its
origins. Post-culturalism on the other hand is a condition, a
state of affairs, not an ideology and least of all a program. It
is not in itself cosmopolitan, pluralistic, tolerant, libertarian, open to change, any more than multiculturalism is always backward-looking or in constant search of traditional
authorities. Post-culturalism is only potentially and inconsistently those things. Its implications are much deeper
than the divisions of party politics in modern democracies,
and therefore only debatably political. For all this necessary
hedging, though, post-culturalism has many implications
for how collective life will change early in the third millennium, in North America and throughout the world.

For at least a hundred years the United States has been
a much more unified country than Canada, but the history
of multiculturalism here has many parallels with the Cana-

dian experience. It only looks different because most American multiculturalists draw on the rhetoric of the civil rights movement, of which they misleadingly consider their own movement a continuation. (Once again, people who aggressively use the word *culture* are usually talking about something else.) First there were blacks—the term *African American* is itself a later product of multiculturalism—to be liberated from what no one doubts was a history of real oppression. Part of that liberation included the early stages of affirmative action. Here, as in Canada, the familiar process soon began of other groups—ethnic or otherwise—insisting on the similarity of their own experience to blacks' and demanding the same kinds of reparation. Where skin color or other obvious evidence of disadvantage was lacking, multiculturalism made it plausible to identify culture as both the target of oppression and the object to be preserved or, if necessary, revived. Bilingualism, first for Spanish-speaking immigrants and their children, then for any other language group with sufficient numbers, became a national policy as it had in Canada.

Preserving or reviving immigrant cultures in countries where they had not originated proved a never-ending task to which no effort might be equal; hence policies had to be constantly ratcheted up, with constant denunciations of anyone who doubted the value of the enterprise. "Racist" had served the civil rights movement well as an accusation, precisely because racism, once endemic, had come to be widely abhorred—otherwise the charge would have lacked bite. Many multiculturalists borrowed "racist" uncritically as an all-purpose epithet for their adversaries—for example, those who voiced skepticism about the usefulness of bilingual education—thereby further obscuring the differences between race, culture, and political ideology. Generally speaking, a sympathetic press did not question the confusing of these categories and (for example) routinely described the children of racially mixed parents as "bicultural."

Fighting prejudice is not the same thing as fighting the natural processes of history, and the death of cultures in English-speaking North America has not on the whole been brought about by bias. Ignoring this distinction makes it harder, not easier, to combat real prejudice, just as Senator Joseph R. McCarthy's celebrated penchant for labeling every liberal a tool of Stalin made the task of identifying real spies more difficult. Far from being a consequence of bigotry, the decline of cultures may in fact be essential to the ideals of liberty, equality, and inclusiveness that America has been gradually achieving over such a long period of time. "We create an impossible contradiction," Alain Finkielkraut, a contemporary French philosopher, points out, "in seeking to establish rules for welcoming diverse ethnic groups based on principles affirming the primacy of cultural roots."[2]

E pluribus unum, the motto of the United States, means "Out of many one," but the one is a wholly different kind of entity from the many, especially since the melting pot took on the feverish rapidity of a microwave. This postcultural quality of American life was previsioned as long ago as the eighteenth century, when the universality of human nature was a widely accepted axiom and Enlightenment thinkers dismissed as mere provinciality any local forces that stood in their way. If all men are created equal, with certain unalienable rights, and Congress shall make no law respecting an establishment of religion, and the golden door remains more or less open, there is not much chance for any culture to preserve its unique qualities or sense of natural superiority by repelling outside influences.

The assertion of the value of diverse cultures and ethnic identities against a supracultural rationalism, or against "a liberal pluralism discourse of ethical universals—freedom, tolerance, charity" that some multiculturalists[3] denounce, is today associated with the left. Historically it belongs to the right. The preciousness of varying cultural traditions and the meaninglessness of natural rights constitute two of the founding doctrines of modern conservatism, in the contemporary-sounding reaction of such eighteenth-century thinkers as Johann Gottfried Herder and Edmund Burke to the Enlightenment and later to the French Revolution. As Isaiah Berlin wrote of Herder in 1964:

> No writer has stressed more vividly the damage done to human beings by being torn from the only conditions in which their history has made it possible for them to live full lives. He insists over and over again that no one milieu or group or way of life is necessarily superior to any other; but it is what it is, and assimilation to a single universal pattern, of laws or language or social structure, as advocated by the French *lumières*, would destroy what is most living and valuable in life and art. . . . Every group has a right to be happy in its own

way. It is terrible arrogance to affirm that, to be happy, everyone should become European.[4]

If every culture has its own traditions (political, social, and otherwise) that are as valid as those of any other, then not only does no basis exist for criticizing another culture from outside—the familiar doctrine of cultural relativism—but there is equally no vantage point from which a minority of its members can demand fundamental change from within. "We are," wrote Burke in *Reflections on the Revolution in France*, "afraid to put men to live and trade each on his own private stock of reason, because we suspect that this stock in each man is small, and that the individuals would do better to avail themselves of the general bank and capital of nations and of ages." Instead of exploding prejudices, intellectuals should seek "to discover the latent wisdom which prevails in them. . . . Prejudice renders a man's virtue his habit, and not a series of unconnected acts. Through just prejudice, his duty becomes a part of his nature."[5] Even in its least attractive manifestations, Burke asserts that culture must be protected against the destructive power of an abstract rationality or theory of justice. Some of the multiculturalists quoted earlier would clearly agree.

Conversely, the universal ideals associated with the American and French revolutions, which Burke and his successors denounced—a belief in self-evident truths or the Rights of Man based on a human nature that is fundamentally the same everywhere—represent a powerful basis for criticism and change in all cultures, not just a few. The multiculturalist defense of diverse cultures, when it goes so

far as denying the validity of universal truths or virtues, attacking the very conception of human nature, would be recognized as profoundly reactionary if it were much more
than a nostalgic attempt to revive the vanishing past—a
thoroughly pick-and-choose procedure that largely ignores
whatever cultural traditions are incompatible with late
twentieth-century progressive values. Its mirror image is the
Christian right, which seeks to restore the authority it
thinks small-town communitarianism, Protestant morality,
and nuclear families had in the mid-nineteenth century.

Although multiculturalism and family values remain
politically resonant doctrines, each with a base in one of the
major American political parties, neither of these backward-
looking movements has achieved much success in its own
terms. In Burke's time, two hundred years ago, it was just
barely possible to be an essentially non-ideological adherent
of the traditions and institutions bequeathed by the past to
one's society, whether British, French, Tibetan, or Zulu.
Today this kind of culture-based conservatism is impossible
even in the world's most stable countries. Every tradition
has been ruptured, every institution opened to question, if
not by revolution then by changes that have undermined its
authority. Whatever attitude one takes toward the religious,
social, or political elements of one's own culture involves
individual choices. There is no longer the possibility of
spontaneous, unthinking acceptance beyond the age of
childhood because there are simply too many options.

One result of all these choices in America was that
starting in the late 1960s politics became, rhetorically at
least, more ideological about a grab bag of "cultural" issues.

The phrase "culture wars" became a commonplace description of what was at issue in congressional elections or a presidential impeachment—above all in the education of children. Meanwhile much of the public predictably grew even more alienated from politics of any sort. Mainstream commentators and elected politicians today try to escape this heightened ideological tension by describing themselves or those they admire as moderates, but the moderation they praise has no content of its own, being defined entirely by the extremes it repudiates. Most politicians and political commentators today are at best dimly aware of a history in which left and right have largely traded positions on cultural issues, but some of the confusions in American politics today are the direct result of it.

Conservatism in the late twentieth century became an unstable amalgam of liberal individualism, patriotism, religiously based morality, nostalgia for a more personal small-town America, and the worship of high technology. Its supposed opposite, the progressive ideology of education and the major communications media, was equally divided between past and future, between the desire to see old prejudices die and the wish to revive lost identities, the determination to advance freedom of discourse and at the same time to forbid words that might offend any group; most self-deceptively of all, to believe that American society was growing more rather than less culturally varied. Each side in this "cultural" debate could be defined by a symbolic position left over from the 1960s. For the right, it was using the power of the government to forbid defacing the American flag, the emblem of national unity that had been a common target of protesters during the Vietnam War. For the left, it was using that same power to enforce "diversity," the proportional representation of racial and ethnic groups in all areas of life, even as those groups were blurring irretrievably through assimilation and intermarriage. Both sides seemed blind to much of what had been happening for thirty years under their noses.

Today North American governments at every level repeat multicultural slogans and hail the "gorgeous mosaic" that has supposedly replaced the melting pot. But what kind of government, what combination of policies could actually achieve the goals of multiculturalism? As the last chapter argued, true diversity cannot exist without liberty for individuals and the groups they belong to. On the other hand, it long ago became doubtful that even the strongest group identities could survive a high degree of individual freedom and opportunity where once separated groups share the same society on a daily basis. Aware of this difficulty, the creators of the Canadian territory of Nunavut seriously considered making only Inuits eligible to vote or hold office there. Even this measure might not have sufficed. How long will the Inuits remain the majority in their immense territory unless the national government forbids anyone else to settle there, in effect turning the place into a heavily subsidized reservation?

The loss of cultural or ethnic identity disorients. It releases some inhibitions and strengthens others, leads to a search for other kinds of identity (through a supra-ethnic nationalism, through identification with sports teams, with products, an occupation, a sex, sex itself) or an artificial reassertion of the identity that has been lost. Freedom, as always, ripens a jumble of fruits. But there is probably no going back.

Controversy over the language of education and everyday life has become a political issue in many countries because individuals' freedom to choose an identity threatens to make the collective past unrecoverable. Remember the prototypical case of Quebec, whose assertion of cultural rights gave rise to multiculturalism in the first place. There the freedom of individuals or families to choose their own medium of expression has been explicitly restricted in order to arrest the decline of French-Canadian language and culture. Left to their own devices, the provincial government fears, its subjects would rapidly embrace English as their primary language and abandon all but the most innocuous features of Quebecois heritage. French-Canadian pea soup would probably survive, but any vigorous sense of nationhood would soon die out. *"Je me souviens,"* the motto printed on every Quebec license plate, would lose all its significance in English. It would be like Texans remembering the Alamo in Spanish.

The cultural nationalism of others produces a deep ambivalence among multiculturalists. On the one hand, they usually believe in tolerance and freedom of choice. On the other hand, in common with most Western intellectuals, they hate to see Chinese or Iranian youths wandering aimlessly around in sweatshirts bearing the names of American colleges, eating Big Macs while listening to American-style popular music on their Walkmen. "McWorld," writes Benjamin Barber, "is a product of popular culture driven by expansionist commerce. Its template is American, its form style. Its goods are as much images as matériel, an aesthetic as well as a product line. It is about culture as commodity, apparel as ideology."[6]

Most intellectuals (up to a point I include myself) would prefer to see non-Western peoples maintain their own cultures, not borrow ours quite so enthusiastically. We like the idea of diversity in the world; we think there should be robust alternatives to the American way of life and that foreigners should have the sense to choose them voluntarily. *McWorld* sums up in a single brilliant coinage what we dislike most about our own society when we meet it abroad. Don't get us wrong; we don't mean the Chinese should go on practicing female infanticide, or that the people of India should remain divided into castes, or that the Muslim world should keep women in veils, or that arranged marriages and authoritarian governments are a good thing. We have less patience than traditional cultures do for poverty, inequality, dirt, disease, overpopulation. But we love to visit ancient temples and picturesque villages; we have a highly cultivated taste for oriental and Mexican and Near Eastern food; we find lots of interesting traditional art for sale in all these destinations. We habitually project on "indigenous" cultures the opposites of all the qualities we dislike in our own society: in Arizona or Bali or Brazil, the original inhabitants are peaceful, noncompetitive, environmentally sound, and sexually liberated.

We fail to see why everyone in the world needs to be as materialistic as other Americans (not ourselves) are. We hate the consumer society at home and wish foreigners would do a better job of proving they agree with us. We feel reassured to know that many Western-educated third world intellectuals agree—those who fearlessly denounce American capitalist hegemony and are punished with professorships at Ivy League universities. But the ordinary third world peoples back home seem to be letting them—and us—down. (Just like our own ordinary people.) After expending so much effort to drive Christmas celebrations out of the American public square in the interests of diversity, we feel betrayed to discover that in Japan and even China— an officially atheistic Communist country—Christmas has become a major holiday, complete with cards and trees and turkeys. The non-Western peoples of the world should have the grace to protect their culture from ours for everyone's sake. Many Western intellectuals feel hopelessly ambivalent about foreign cultures because they feel so critical toward their own. This ambivalence is the taproot of scholarly multiculturalism. The secret (neither little nor dirty) is that academic multiculturalism has less to do with other cultures than with the relation of European and American intellectuals to their own societies.

From the 1960s on, and increasingly in the 1980s, Marxist revolutionary movements in Latin America, whose origins had little to do with ethnicity, learned to wrap them-

selves in the mantle of indigenous identities allegedly suppressed for five hundred years by Spanish and then American imperialism. The uprising in the Mexican state of
Chiapas and the fictionalized autobiography of the
Guatemalan leftist Rigoberta Menchú, which helped win
her the Nobel Peace Prize in 1992 and remains a best-seller
in European and American academic circles, demonstrate
the continuing appeal of multicultural revolutionary rhetoric to gullible professors. My point is not that no justification exists for radical change in these societies. It is rather
that the realities of guerrilla movements, their causes and
effects, are deliberately obscured behind the attractive
mask of the stereotypical Indian victim. Few third world
revolutionaries need to be told that these days cultural
genocide makes a more effective international rallying cry
than the class struggle.[7]

Latin American revolution is a minority taste today in
North American universities, but the way its devotees market it illustrates a far more prevalent unease about the future of cultures. Travelers abroad have been complaining
for a long time that the whole world is starting to look the
same. After World War II it was the Americanization of Europe. The French Academy has been trying unsuccessfully
to stamp out *Franglais* since the 1950s. The Communist
world soon came up with a slogan for what was going on:
cultural imperialism. Now that most Communist regimes,
with the massive exception of China's, have succumbed to
the very phenomena under examination, a new, seemingly
more neutral coinage has taken hold: globalization (a

process), or globalism (an outlook). Whole books have been written deploring the popularity of American consumer goods in Asia and Africa—by 1994 Beijing already had the busiest McDonald's in the world, with Tokyo and Moscow not far behind—and breathlessly wondering where it will all lead. "Does the spread of fast food undermine the integrity of indigenous cuisines?" asks James L. Watson, the anthropologist. "Are food chains helping to create a homogeneous, global culture better suited to the needs of a capitalist world order?"[8]

Globalization abroad sorts opinions—sometimes violently—along exactly the same lines as the decline of cultures in North America. As Salman Rushdie noted in the same *New York Times* article quoted earlier, "The globalizing power of American culture is opposed by an improbable alliance that includes everyone from cultural-relativist liberals to hard-line fundamentalists, with all manner of pluralists and individualists, to say nothing of flag-waving nationalists and splintering sectarians, in between." Libertarians, managers of large corporations, and the world's teenagers—another improbable alliance—tend to love it. A middle group, represented by Barber, condemns both globalization and its contrary, strong "cultural" identities that enforce conformity on their members. His most important charge is that both extremes reduce democracy, which he associates with an idealized community of ethnic groups in which historical identities are not a source of conflict. "Neither Jihad nor McWorld," he charges, "aspires to resecure the civic virtues undermined by its denationalizing practices; neither global markets nor blood communities service public goods or pursue equality and justice. . . . Jihad pursues a bloody politics of identity, McWorld a bloodless economics of profit."[9]

Is the process of globalization, then, the same thing as post-culturalism, and are we on the brink of a post-cultural world? Capitalism and democracy were originally products of Western European history but are now almost universal aspirations because they seem to satisfy so many demands of people in widely different cultures. As Barber suggests, globalization tends at first to be conceived not in political but in economic terms, with the English language and the icons of American popular culture following in its wake. The most common meaning of globalization is a set of financial arrangements beginning with free trade and open capital markets, possibly (Barber is not alone in his skepticism) encouraging the transition to democracy as an eventual bonus. Whatever else it may be, it is not a culture or, in Max Lerner's terminology, a civilization. Nor, on the other hand, does its advance through the world necessarily portend the extinction of cultures. Even Watson, suspicious of the transnational capitalism so successfully represented by McDonald's, describes the achievement of a single global culture as "essentially impossible" and considers the homogenizing effects of American products on the world overstated.[10]

In 1996 the Harvard political scientist Samuel P. Huntington published an intensely gloomy book entitled *The Clash of Civilizations and the Remaking of World Order*. Expanding on articles and speeches that had earlier made the outlines of his thesis notorious, Huntington argued that far from exhibiting either a world civilization or a universalizing global order, the end of the millennium was a time when cultural identities on the grand scale had replaced ideology as the principal basis for conflict.

> The post–Cold War world is a world of seven or eight major civilizations. Cultural commonalities and differences shape the interests, antagonisms, and associations of states. The most important countries in the world come overwhelmingly from different civilizations. The local conflicts most likely to escalate into broader wars are those between groups and states from different civilizations.

Once the cold war ceased to divide members of the same civilizations along ideological lines, all Serbs or all Chinese, all Turks or all Albanians inevitably sought to unite in the kind of culturally based superstate that has come to be known as Greater Serbia or Greater China. "Power," Huntington adds ominously, "is shifting from the long predominant West to non-Western civilizations."[11]

For Huntington, a multicultural America offers no solution to these cultural conflicts. Nor does traditional Western universalism. In fact, both these ideas represent dangers to Americans because "Both deny the uniqueness of Western culture," and the only way for a civilization to hold its own in such a strife-torn world is by maintaining its specificity as strongly as possible: "The preservation of the United States and the West requires the renewal of Western identity." Paradoxically, he believes, this renewal would make possible global multiculturalism, or the more or less peaceful coexistence of distinct civilizations in a world that no civilization is powerful enough to dominate. "Cultures," Huntington declares epigrammatically, "are relative; morality is absolute. . . . In a multicivilizational world, the constructive course is to renounce universalism, accept diversity, and seek commonalities."[12]

How the "commonalities" of an absolute morality differ from universalism remains something of a mystery, with the result that Huntington's attempt to pay due respect to differences while resisting the traps of cultural relativism is unpersuasive. How could it be otherwise, given his emphasis on the persistence of warring cultures? Like so many aspects of the modern world, the conflicts he identifies could be explained in quite different ways by an observer with less reverence for the idea of culture. One could easily argue, for example, that "Greater Serbia" and "Greater Albania," perhaps even "Greater China," represent not civilizations seeking completeness but provincial forms of the nineteenth-century nationalism described by Isaiah Berlin. In mounting his attack on what was rapidly becoming a dominant model of globalization, however, Huntington made a powerful case that any notion of an emerging world civilization—let alone of a radically Westernizing world—was, at the very least, premature.

The fate of Kremlinology—the study of the Soviet Union—teaches us that no scholarly discipline is much good at predicting the future of the world. Too many factors are involved. Anyone who tries to explain something as complicated as the global evolution of cultures is thrown back on common sense and a host of suppositions. Dressing up a forecast of dubious origins in the academic equivalent of white tie and tails is merely the accepted scholarly way to deceive both oneself and the poor bewildered reader. Bearing all that in mind, we must now turn our attention to the planet's future, briefly and without further expressions of caution.

To state it simply, there are three major interconnected reasons for doubting that most of the world will become fully post-cultural. The first is language. The second is the strength of a major culture on its home ground, unless overwhelmed by conquest and incorporation into another nation. (That seems to be the fate of Tibet.) Combining the effects of these two conservative influences is a third, ideological reason: nationalism.

Language. A particular language is the chief medium through which any culture transmits its teachings. As a barrier to competing cultural forces from outside, it has been peculiarly underestimated. Barber, who fears McWorld and Jihad equally, makes what he considers an especially telling observation:

> Most important, the global culture speaks English—or, better, American. In McWorld's terms, the queen's English is little more today than a highfalutin dialect used by advertisers who want to reach affected upscale American consumers. American English has become

the world's primary transnational language in culture and the arts as well as in science, technology, commerce, transportation, and banking. The debate over whether America or Japan has seized global leadership is conducted in English. . . . The war against the hard hegemony of American colonialism, political sovereignty, and economic empire is fought in a way that advances the soft hegemony of American pop culture and the English language.[13]

Some of this plaint rings true, but it misses the crucial difference between a primary and a second language. Speaking a second language well gives one access to the resources, popular and otherwise, of another culture. It does not in normal circumstances displace one's own.

True, linguists expect about half the world's existing six thousand languages to expire in the twenty-first century. But most of these anticipated casualties belong to tiny, formerly isolated cultures of the sort that Ruth Benedict or Margaret Mead wrote about and are succumbing to Spanish, English, French, Russian, or Chinese. Since major non-English-speaking countries are not likely to abandon their own languages, the most distinctive features of their cultures can probably resist the worst that McWorld has to offer in the way of deep transformation, provided immigration does not overwhelm them. There is, however, a corollary to the general rule of linguistic exclusivity. Of all the world's tongues, English has gone farthest toward losing its associations with a particular culture and ethnicity. Even as a primary language it has the most widely dispersed and varied speakers and writers; for at least a century and a half most of its native speakers have lived outside the British Isles. For similar reasons having to do with a colonial empire and its aftermath, Spanish is almost equally disjoined from its Iberian origins. Chinese, French, and Russian retain much more powerful associations with the originating country and culture. Other things being equal, their speakers should be more resistant to the deeper cultural effects of globalization than people in lands where English or Spanish is dominant.

No matter which non-English language is at issue, however, American supporters of bilingual education are quite correct, given their desire to preserve immigrant cultures here, to insist that the children under their control should continue to speak their parents' language. If they learn English with difficulty as a second language and always speak it as if it were foreign to them, so much the better. As primary language goes, so goes culture, whether in New York, Quebec, or Beijing. The power of a language to transmit a culture and filter out the less superficial aspects of competing cultures is of course all the greater where its majority status is unchallenged. As long as France speaks French and China speaks Chinese, globalization will never totally displace their native cultures, though it will certainly influence their natural evolution. That influence brings us to

The persistence of a culture on its native turf. In North America, all but a minute fraction of the population descends from people who recently came from somewhere else. Every culture was foreign here, faced with an unfamiliar environment. Except for the small proportion of WASPs, practically all United States residents speak a language that they or their ancestors learned after they arrived. Whatever countries they came from had cultures that evolved in a particular geographical and historical setting, usually quite different from the one that immigrants encountered here. As well as an unfamiliar landscape, they confronted a set of ideals—life, liberty, the pursuit of happiness, paddle your own canoe—that were the secular religion of their new country. Whether those ideals helped bring them here in the first place or later took them by surprise, nearly all immigrant autobiographies talk about them at length. This set of circumstances was tailor-made for post-culturalism.

Suppose they had stayed home. In places such as France or China their individual and collective experiences would have been entirely different. They would have kept their language, their relatives, their neighbors, their schools, their monuments, their customs large and small, their furniture. Their lives still would have been changed out of recognition over the past century by war, revolution, and economic modernization, but the experience would not have been anything like living in a new country surrounded by people from everywhere under the sun. Eventually America would have affected them even at home—militarily, economically, through the power of its ideals—but affected them as French or Chinese, not as Americans. The result would be what in fact it is: a degree of hybridization, a set of new choices, a blending of influences to produce dynamic and not wholly predictable mixtures that still differ markedly from one another.

In much the same way, what makes such twentieth-century North American creations as Nunavut or the Navajo Big Reservation something more than ethnic theme parks, despite all their problems, is the fact that the inhabitants have not been uprooted. Although their numbers are minuscule compared with the non-native peoples who now surround them, they still live in the land where their language and way of life originally evolved. Like the fragile cultures anthropologists studied early in the century, Navajo and Inuit approaches to the world have been altering rapidly as their members adapt to overwhelming realities. How long their languages can last as cradle tongues is questionable. Even so, something genuine and worthy of respect survives for the time being.

On other continents, as in North America, post-culturalism is likely to develop furthest and fastest in large, open countries settled by immigrants of widely varying origins—Australia, possibly Argentina. Affluent young tourists from other big, dissimilar societies such as France and China can meet and communicate (probably in English) at any of the world's McDonald's. In that sense they all hold citizenship in McWorld. But at the end of all their travels and transitions they will still be French, still be Chinese, distinct from each other and from Americans. Surfing the web for business or pleasure can increase the points of reference they have in common, as the Catholic religion and the Latin language did for Europeans during the Middle Ages; it will never come close to erasing their cultural differences. Nor will intermarriage across linguistic and national boundaries ever blend their populations to anything like the degree it has been doing in the United States. In the case of such durable, strongly marked historical identities as the French or Chinese, that would be so even without

Nationalism. If twentieth-century history proved anything, it was that economic self-interest is no match for the imperatives of nationalism, however self-destructive. One of the most distressing facts at the turn of the millennium is that in most of the world nationalism has not grown weaker, still less faded away. The number of actual or aspiring nations has been rising steadily as formerly submerged groups—Muslims in the Caucasus, Slovaks, Palestinians, Kosovo Albanians, French Canadians, Kurds—demand independent states in logical consequence of their ethnic uniqueness. States whose justification for existing is the expression of a specific group identity are rarely models of human rights. The collapse of communism as a system of belief has led in many places, as is well known, not to democratic liberties but to the substitute religion of the nation. "Individuals must put the states' rights before their own," the foreign minister of China declared at the World Conference on Human Rights in 1993, repeating an axiom of nationalists old and new.[14]

Today nationalism frequently uses the language of culture, even of academic multiculturalism, not only in the former Yugoslavia but in much of Africa and Asia, where "cultural rights" and the language of Western anthropology rationalize the most backward kinds of repression. Now that claims of racial superiority are taboo, the rhetoric of cultural difference serves the same nationalist purposes and is accepted by many in the West because it sounds so familiar.

179

Alain Finkielkraut describes the transition from one kind of exclusivism to another:

> Those who invented the idea of the national spirit . . . were the first to reject human nature, replacing the concept with the irreducible variety of cultures. . . . The theory of races that came later on *naturalized this rejection of human nature* and, more generally, everything else that might transcend the diversity of cultures. For the proponents of racial theory the specific traits of each people were engraved in the genes; the national "spirits" became quasi species endowed with a hereditary character, permanent and indelible.
>
> We believe we have since discredited the idea of race, but have we really made any progress? Like the racists before them, contemporary fanatics of cultural identity confine individuals to their group of origin. Like them, they carry differences to the absolute extreme, and . . . destroy any possibility of a natural or cultural community among peoples.[15]

None of the universalisms of the eighteenth or twentieth centuries, not the rights of man or internationalism or socialism or globalism, has succeeded in overcoming the narrower collective appeal of nationalism. Nor has the awfulness of modern war, a fact everywhere apparent. The Internet will have no better success. The fact that nationalism has intelligible historical roots in the European reaction to the French Revolution, or that extreme nationalist movements throughout the world usually follow the same patterns, is not much comfort. Diagnosis is not the same as cure, still less as inoculation. Does China's ancient civilization lead inexorably to dictatorship and periodic bouts of rage at "foreign devils"? Can Serbian culture really be as murderous as it seemed throughout the 1990s? Probably not, any more than German culture inevitably led to genocide and the pursuit of a "Greater Germany." But the same xenophobic model repeats itself with depressing frequency.

Yesterday—caricatured, rigidified, reshaped in the language of cultural autonomy to serve present-day purposes—is still a great power in the eponymous home of Balkanization and throughout much of the non-European world. Outside the closed group, there are still no human beings. The homicidal ruthlessness of Indonesian or Serbian nationalism suggests identities that feel gravely threatened, but there seems little reason to predict that they will share the fate of immigrant cultures in the United States. The survival of languages and nations assures, for better or worse, that globalization has natural limits well short of a post-cultural world. Tomorrow when it comes will not look the same in Africa or the Caucasus as it does in Los Angeles.

The great exception may be Western Europe, the civilization that tore itself apart in two world wars and is now trying to bind itself together so tightly that war between Germany and France will be as impossible as between Missouri and Kansas. The only way to get rid of nationalism, the most influential European leaders seem to believe, is by getting rid of nations. For fifty years they have worked away at it with uncountable commissions and regulations and studies and plans and calculations of every imaginable kind. Both the hopes and the ironies are worth attention, if only because the contradictions involved are so instructive. In an era of multiculturalism, a policy to which all its nations officially subscribe, the European Union (EU) moves toward a federation that irons out all serious differences of economic, political, and social policy on the grounds that Europe fought two world wars in this century and can no longer afford to be diverse in anything that really counts. To insure against a third world war, its leaders have already developed a customs union, a common currency and central bank, freedom of residency throughout the Union, increasingly a single supergovernment, in practice perhaps a single *lingua franca*, which realistically can only be English, the language of business.

At the birth of the Euro currency in 1999, CBS News hailed its advantages by demonstrating that for the first time European travelers could easily compare the price of blue jeans, the uniform of American youth culture, in Berlin and Rome. For everyone concerned, the United States was the explicit standard of comparison. Not only would all this downplaying of national cultures prevent another world war (the claim went), it would also strengthen economic competition with the United States. Meanwhile, European national and regional authorities continually celebrate the blandest, least divisive aspects of local cultural traditions: food, picturesque costumes, peasant dialects in Britain or Bavaria that will soon die out unless the schools inculcate them. In the EU as in McWorld, the mass production and marketing of everything across national borders reduces both cultural identity and individualism. So much for multiculturalism of any depth.

But even Euroland will never be fully post-cultural, for all its desire to get along with itself. That would require not just an end to nations and nationalism but an authoritarian uprooting of languages and cultures beyond anything seen in history over such a wide area. In seventy years of ruthless, often murderous effort, the Soviet Union never managed to stamp out non-Russian tongues and ways of life in its empire. Why should humane Europe be tempted to try such an experiment? Languages and cultures cause no wars in themselves. For two hundred years nationalism has been the culprit. Whether getting rid of so much national independence was necessary to prevent war seems questionable, but anyone with a sense of history can understand why the leaders of Germany, who propelled the project, felt reluctant to take any more chances. Still, merging a dozen economies and discrediting nationalism fall well short of obliterating the residue of national cultures. The contradictions of the process actually strengthen impulses toward secession in such places as Scotland and Languedoc, where local patriots dream of reviving once distinct languages and traditions within the framework of a united Europe.

There is no telling how European centralization will work out in the middle to long run, or whether other troubled parts of the world (Latin America, East Asia, the Arab world) may eventually follow Europe's lead. Again, no academic discipline has a big enough crystal ball. For all the attempts of the concerned governments to control every factor and smother every contingency with regulations and bureaucracy, the biggest questions about Europe's future are not directly subject to anyone's power, individual or collective, political or economic or cultural. European premiers and foreign observers alike can only wait and see what emerges now that every *i* is buried in dots and every *t* exhibits half a century of crosses.

The unpredictability of cultural or political change—history's bad habit of doing things without informing us in advance—is as unsettling to scholars as it is to statesmen. For one thing, it makes scholarship about the present a risky commitment; think again of all those Kremlinologists who never expected their subject matter to go out of business. But another major reason exists for scholars with certain political commitments to grumble about unplanned, spontaneous change: it seems, and is, completely undemocratic. The worst thing about both Jihad and McWorld, Barber complains, is that "squeezed between their opposing forces, the world has been sent spinning out of control. Can it be that what Jihad and McWorld have in common is anarchy: the absence of common will and that conscious and collective human control under the guidance of law we call democracy?"[16]

Of course, we might ask just whose conscious control the world was under before these developments spun it into anarchy. Nonetheless it would be hard to deny that the contest between culture and post-culturalism, of which Jihad and McWorld could be regarded as caricatures, is mostly outside anyone's control. Profound cultural changes normally occur not without human agency but by the agency of so many human beings who are spontaneously living their

lives—marrying or emigrating, choosing a religion or an occupation, affirming or rejecting an old identity—that no
public authority can plan them. Something so amorphous
as the future of culture, even in a single large country, can
rarely become a coherent political issue because the most
powerful or far-seeing government has so little power over
it. Unquestionably post-cultural individualism, with its ignorance of and contempt for politics, does weaken "that
conscious and collective human control under the guidance
of law we call democracy," in Barber's words. But there
would be narrow limits in any event to what politics could
accomplish in this sphere. The openness of the cultural future, humbling to scholars and governments alike, contains
a mixture of threats and opportunities for everyone—a plat-
itude, but worth remembering all the same.

Summing up the lessons of his country's calamitous devotion to Jihad, a Kosovo Serb named Radovan Delibasic
told the *New York Times* (July 2, 1999): "We have learned
that you cannot live from history. Americans have no history
and they live wonderfully well." Probably so philosophical a
refugee knew that Americans *do* have a history. What he
most likely meant was that their history imposes on living
Americans no crushing burden of ethnic identity or inherited duty to purge the land of others regardless of cost. The
world still has much to learn from America because Americans have learned so many hard lessons from the world.
Even so, is it any surprise that America's problems of free-

dom and identity take strikingly different forms from those of Europe, let alone the non-European world? The rash promises of 1776, together with the unending struggle they engendered over how faithfully they needed to be kept, produced a society unlike any other and (sometimes) progeny that even the boldest Founding Father would have disowned. No other large country has ever been so open to outsiders. No other country has so undermined, through its founding ideals and actual ways of life, the identities of those who lived there. By gradually turning more and more categories of outsiders into insiders, a process without logical limit, America began to solve some of the oldest problems of humanity while systematically dismantling the whole basis of traditional cultures. For when everyone belongs, there is no "other" left for a culture to define itself against.

Contemplating the graveyard of cultures that was such a spectacular consequence of the founders' words, one can only hope that the post-cultural way of life, as it continues to evolve, will achieve greater depth and spontaneous order. The standard alternatives to it grow weaker every year and were always less attractive than they seem to their enthusiasts. In the contested suburbs of social ideology, multiculturalism on the left and monoculturalism on the right flourish deceptively as expressions of longing for a past—differently interpreted, of course—that has drifted beyond recovery. At bottom they both mean living in a museum. Polls and other evidence suggest that most Americans regard the breakdown of families and communities with a sensible dismay, but no form of political action is likely to restore those institutions' health. Similarly with a host of imperatives that used to be conspicuous in American life. The problem is not so much competition from other ideals, still less from other cultures, as it is the weakening of all normative standards of behavior and judgment, no matter what their source. To say that this far-reaching evolutionary process has ambiguous results is an understatement, but those who hope to master it by an act of will are courting disappointment.

Whatever fresh surprises history has in store, we seem likely to go on traveling the information highways in a post-cultural direction for a good while, whether we like it or not. Now that most of the old guideposts have rotted away, will individuals who have been emancipated from every authority but their own personalities start to rediscover some stronger basis for harmony and mutual respect than a bland refusal to judge? How comforting it would be to imagine a future in which the best features of America after cultures—individual freedom made truly universal, the self-confidence that comes from social equality, an openness to outside influences, a refusal to perpetuate ancient quarrels—had prevailed and its worst features gradually disappeared. But the negative qualities of the post-cultural condition are a deformed version of the good ones—the sentimental narcissism of those who recognize no demand but self-satisfaction, emotional exhibitionism, a substitute religion of products and celebrities, a smug indifference to the causes of conflict in the world. Most likely neither set of qualities will prevail over the other. They are simply too intertwined.

"Be not disheartened," Walt Whitman, the prophet of an all-inclusive America liberated from the historic demands of culture, prophesied just before the Civil War, "affection shall solve the problems of freedom yet." It would be encouraging to think so, or at least to hope, at a time when freedom leads in such confusing directions. Much of the world is a different story; exorcising ghostly identities in the haunted nations where they still imprison and murder is another order of problem that will probably require stronger solutions. But even this sorry conclusion should reassure us that the dilemmas of freedom are infinitely preferable to the sleepwalking certainties of unfreedom, and a nation that spends its history struggling with them is fortunate beyond any historical precedent.

Notes

Introduction: Freedom and Nostalgia

1. Max Lerner, *America as a Civilization* (New York: Simon and Schuster, 1957), p. 59. (Subsequent quotations are from pages 56–57, 60, 61, 81, and 93.)

2. As I discovered after employing it in this sense, the word has been used before, though it appears in no dictionary. Some practitioners of critical theory have used it to refer to a stage or version of their discipline that succeeds cultural studies.

3. Nathan Glazer, *We Are All Multiculturalists Now* (Cambridge, Mass.: Harvard University Press, 1997), p. 161.

4. *1998 Report on Television* (New York: Nielsen Media Research, 1998), p. 17. The total number of hours that television is turned on in the average household has risen only slightly since the mid-1950s. See Charles S. Aaronson, ed., *1956 International Television Almanac* (New York: Quigley Publications, 1956), p. xii.

The most significant difference is that now even people over fifty-five—the age group that spends longest in front of the set—have been watching it since childhood.

Chapter 1. The Cult of "Culture"

1. Gary Chapman, "Net Gain," *New Republic*, July 31, 1995, pp. 10, 12.

2. John R. Levine, Carol Baroudi, and Margaret Levine Young, *The Internet for Dummies*, 3rd ed. (Foster City, Calif.: IDG Books, 1996), p. 11.

3. Margaret Mead, 1959 Preface to Ruth Benedict, *Patterns of Culture* (New York: Mentor Books, 1959; first published 1934), p. v.

4. Sir Edward Burnett Tylor, *The Origins of Culture* (vol. I of *Primitive Culture*) (New York: Harper, 1958), p. 1.

5. Benedict, *Patterns of Culture*, pp. 18, 22.

6. Alfred Kroeber, *The Nature of Culture* (Chicago: University of Chicago Press, 1952), p. 6.

7. Quoted in Amartya Sen, "Human Rights and Asian Values," *New Republic*, July 14–21, 1997, p. 33.

8. Jack Donnelly, *Universal Human Rights in Theory and Practice* (Ithaca: Cornell University Press, 1989), pp. 119–120.

9. Benedict, *Patterns of Culture*, p. 220; George P. Murdock, "The Common Denominator of Cultures," in Ralph Linton, ed., *The Science of Man in the World Crisis* (New York: Columbia University Press, 1945), p. 124. Murdock adds that "Early reports of peoples lacking language or fire, morals or religion, marriage or government, have been proved erroneous in every instance" (p. 123) and "In all societies the nuclear family is established by marriage, and the relationship between its adult members is characterized by a division of labor according to sex" (p. 140).

10. Franz Boas, *Anthropology and Modern Life* (New York: Norton, 1932), pp. 245–246. "In recognizing the ubiquity of cultural change and the importance of its analysis," wrote another prominent interwar anthropologist, "it must not be forgotten that,

as in any aspect of the study of culture, the phenomenon exists in terms of setting and background, and not by and of itself. This is why a discussion of change in culture has meaning only as part of the problem of cultural stability." Melville J. Herskovits, "The Processes of Cultural Change," in Linton, *Science of Man*, p. 144.

11. Introduction, James L. Watson, ed., *Golden Arches East: McDonald's in East Asia* (Stanford: Stanford University Press, 1997), p. 8.

12. Anne Fadiman, *The Spirit Catches You and You Fall Down* (New York: Farrar, Straus and Giroux, 1997), p. 28.

13. Ibid., p. 276. Emphasis in original.

14. Kathryn Hopkins Kavanagh and Patricia H. Kennedy, *Promoting Cultural Diversity: Strategies for Health-Care Professionals* (Newbury Park, Calif.: Sage Publications, 1992), pp. 5, 24.

15. On cultural studies and science, see Paul R. Gross and Norman Levitt, *Higher Superstition: The Academic Left and Its Quarrels with Science* (Baltimore: Johns Hopkins University Press, 1994) and Alan Sokal and Jean Bricmont, *Fashionable Nonsense: Postmodern Philosophers' Abuse of Science* (New York: Picador, 1998).

16. Michael Polanyi, "On the Modern Mind," *Encounter*, 24 (May 1965), p. 19.

17. Kroeber, *Nature of Culture*, p. 6.

18. Benedict, *Patterns of Culture*, p. 29.

19. Ibid., p. 30.

20. Jon Krakauer, *Into Thin Air* (New York: Villard Books, 1997), pp. 45–46.

21. Sigmund Freud, *Civilization and Its Discontents*, Standard Edition of the Complete Psychological Works of Sigmund Freud, tr. James Strachey, XXI (London: Hogarth, 1962), p. 114.

Chapter 2. Multiculturalism as Museum

1. U.S. Bureau of the Census, Table 5. Detailed Language Spoken at Home and Ability to Speak English for Persons 5 Years and Over, 1990, Internet release date February 18, 1998; Table 2.

Selected Characteristics of the Foreign-born Population by Year of Entry: March 1997, Internet release date April 9, 1998. By the time of the next update, released on September 17, 1999, the total foreign-born percentage had dropped to 9.3. Available at the bureau's website, www.census.gov.

2. Glenn Loury, "Double Talk," *New Republic,* August 25, 1997, p. 23.

3. Benjamin Barber, *A Place for Us* (New York: Hill and Wang, 1998), pp. 29–30.

4. Mary C. Waters, *Ethnic Options: Choosing Identities in America* (Berkeley: University of California Press, 1990), p. 14.

5. Charles Taylor, "The Politics of Recognition," in Amy Gutmann, ed., *Multiculturalism: Examining the Politics of Recognition* (Princeton: Princeton University Press, 1994), pp. 52–53.

6. Terence Turner, "Anthropology and Multiculturalism: What Is Anthropology That Multiculturalists Should Be Mindful of It?" in David Theo Goldberg, ed., *Multiculturalism: A Critical Reader* (Oxford: Blackwell, 1994), p. 407.

7. Peter McLaren, "White Terror and Oppositional Agency: Towards a Critical Multiculturalism," in Goldberg, *Multiculturalism,* pp. 51, 53.

8. Margaret Talbot, "Baghdad on the Plains," *New Republic,* August 11–28, 1997, p. 21.

9. See Theodora Kroeber, *Ishi in Two Worlds: A Biography of the Last Wild Indian in North America* (Berkeley: University of California Press, 1961).

10. David Hollinger, *Postethnic America* (New York: Basic Books, 1995), p. 46.

11. Glazer, *All Multiculturalists Now,* pp. 13–14.

12. Alan Wolfe, *One Nation After All* (New York: Viking Press, 1998), p. 157.

13. Ibid., pp. 159, 160.

14. Anthony Appiah, "Identity, Authenticity, Survival: Multicultural Societies and Social Reproduction," in Gutmann, *Multiculturalism,* pp. 149, 155.

15. Hollinger, *Postethnic America,* pp. 154, 161.

16. Wolfe, *One Nation,* p. 54.

17. Ibid., p. 299.

18. Peter Caws, "Identity: Cultural, Transcultural, and Multicultural," in Goldberg, *Multiculturalism*, p. 381.

19. Steven Rockefeller, "Comment," in Gutmann, *Multiculturalism*, p. 94.

20. Susan Wolf, "Comment," in Gutmann, *Multiculturalism*, pp. 81–83.

21. Christine Chapman, "Granny Dolls Tell Tales of Days Gone By," *Modern Maturity*, September–October 1998, p. 84.

Chapter 3. Intermarriage and the 2050 Fallacy

1. Philip Young, *Three Bags Full: Essays in American Fiction* (New York: Harcourt, Brace, 1973), p. 178.

2. John J. Miller, *The Unmaking of Americans* (New York: Free Press, 1998), p. 145. Detailed information on state miscegenation statutes is given in Paul R. Spickard, *Mixed Blood* (Madison: University of Wisconsin Press, 1989), pp. 374–375.

3. Sources for the figures in the two preceding paragraphs are U.S. Bureau of the Census, *Statistical Abstract of the United States*, 118th ed. (Washington, D.C.: Government Printing Office, 1998), p. 60, table 67; *1999 World Almanac and Book of Facts*, p. 877; Miller, *Unmaking of Americans*, pp. 144–145; "Can Intermarriage Make You Smarter and Richer?" from STATS (Statistical Assessment Service) website newsletter, August 1997 (www.stats.org/newsletters). Articles that shed light on some of these figures appeared in the *New Democrat* for August 1996, *Society* for September 1997, and *National Journal* for January 16, 1999.

4. Gabrielle Glaser, *Strangers to the Tribe* (Boston: Houghton Mifflin, 1997), p. xii.

5. William Sander, "Catholicism and Intermarriage in the United States," *Journal of Marriage and the Family*, 55:4 (1993), pp. 1038–1039.

6. Spickard, *Mixed Blood*, pp. 117, 118.

7. Ibid., p. 117.

8. Glaser, *Strangers to the Tribe*, p. 6.

9. Ibid., p. 70.

10. Caws, "Identity," p. 385.

11. Glaser, *Strangers to the Tribe*, p. 58.

12. Jack Wertheimer, "The Orthodox Moment," *Commentary*, February 1999, p. 19.

13. Glaser, *Strangers to the Tribe*, pp. 64–65.

14. Caws, "Identity," p. 381.

15. Glaser, *Strangers to the Tribe*, p. xiv.

16. Peter Skerry, "Sampling Error," *New Republic*, May 31, 1999, p. 18.

17. The Census Bureau's complete projections for 2050 and other years are available at its website (as are current population estimates). Figures used here are from the revised Projections of the Resident Population by Race, Hispanic Origin, and Nativity: Middle Series, Internet release date January 13, 2000.

18. Amitai Etzioni, "Counting by Race," *City Journal*, Winter 1998, pp. 6, 7; Orlando Patterson, "Race Over," *New Republic*, January 10, 2000, p. 6.

Chapter 4. Mass Individualism and the End of Culture

1. Mao Tse-tung, "On Correcting Mistaken Ideas in the Party," in *Selected Military Writings of Mao Tse-tung* (Peking: Foreign Languages Press, 1963), p. 59.

2. Ralph Waldo Emerson, "Self-Reliance," in Richard Poirier, ed., *Ralph Waldo Emerson* (New York: Oxford University Press, 1990), p. 133.

3. For an explicitly libertarian account of individualism and related issues, see David Boaz, *Libertarianism: A Primer* (New York: Free Press, 1997), especially chapters 2–5. For a recent liberal critique of traditional individualism—one of many—see Jack Crittenden, *Beyond Individualism: Reconstituting the Liberal Self* (New York: Oxford University Press, 1992).

4. Emerson, "Self-Reliance," p. 131; Whitman, "By Blue Ontario's Shore." Other Whitman poems quoted in this chapter and

the next are "One's-Self I Sing" and "Over the Carnage Rose Prophetic a Voice."

5. Emerson, "Self-Reliance," pp. 134, 139.

6. Pierre Manent, "The Modern State," in Mark Lilla, ed., *New French Thought: Political Philosophy* (Princeton: Princeton University Press, 1994), p. 130.

7. Alonzo L. Hamby, *Liberalism and Its Challengers: FDR to Reagan* (New York: Oxford University Press, 1985), p. 342. Anticipating a potential objection, Hamby adds in a note: "One can argue persuasively that Jimmy Carter was more hurt than helped, both as candidate and as president, by his conspicuous Southernness and his pietistic Southern Baptist faith."

8. For a fuller discussion of the related phenomena of personality in contemporary American life and the tabloid press, see Christopher Clausen, *My Life with President Kennedy* (Iowa City: University of Iowa Press, 1994), chapters 2 and 3.

9. H. L. Mencken, *The Vintage Mencken* (New York: Vintage Books, 1955), p. 232.

10. Alexis de Tocqueville, *Democracy in America* (New York: Modern Library, 1981), p. 583.

11. Lerner, *America as a Civilization*, p. 262.

12. John Stuart Mill, *On Liberty*, ed. David Spitz (New York: Norton, 1975), p. 54.

13. Ibid., pp. 57–58.

14. Ibid., pp. 62, 68–69.

15. Ibid., p. 64.

16. Donnelly, *Universal Human Rights*, p. 149.

17. See Alain Finkielkraut, *The Defeat of the Mind* (New York: Columbia University Press, 1995), especially pp. 80–86, and Donnelly, *Universal Human Rights*, pp. 156–158.

Chapter 5. Toward a Post-Cultural World?

1. Isaiah Berlin, "Nationalism," in *The Proper Study of Mankind: An Anthology of Essays* (New York: Farrar, Straus and Giroux, 1998), pp. 590–591.

2. Finkielkraut, *Defeat of the Mind,* p. 93.

3. Robert Stam and Ella Shohat, "Contested Histories: Eurocentrism, Multiculturalism, and the Media," in Goldberg, *Multiculturalism,* p. 300.

4. Berlin, "Herder and the Enlightenment," in *The Proper Study of Mankind,* p. 415.

5. Edmund Burke, *Reflections on the Revolution in France,* ed. J. G. A. Pocock (Indianapolis: Hackett, 1987), pp. 76–77.

6. Benjamin Barber, *Jihad vs. McWorld* (New York: Times Books, 1995), p. 17.

7. See David Stoll, *Rigoberta Menchú and the Story of All Poor Guatemalans* (Boulder, Colo.: Westview Press, 1999).

8. Watson, *Golden Arches East,* pp. 5–6.

9. Barber, *Jihad vs. McWorld,* pp. 7–8. In *The Future and Its Enemies* (New York: Free Press, 1998), Virginia Postrel divides the world in much the same way between "dynamists" and "stasists"; unlike Barber, she enthusiastically endorses the former.

10. Watson, *Golden Arches East,* pp. 7, 8.

11. Samuel P. Huntington, *The Clash of Civilizations and the Remaking of World Order* (New York: Simon and Schuster, 1996), pp. 29, 41, 127.

12. Ibid., p. 318.

13. Barber, *Jihad vs. McWorld,* p. 84.

14. Sen, "Human Rights," p. 33.

15. Finkielkraut, *Defeat of the Mind,* p. 79.

16. Barber, *Jihad vs. McWorld,* p. 5.

Index

Index

Appiah, K. Anthony, 75–76
Argentina, 33, 178
Assimilation, 6–7, 16, 85, 165;
    ambiguities of, 51; and
    blacks, 115–116; failure of,
    9; and identity, 100–110;
    Jewish, 14; and post-
    culturalism, 106–107. *See
    also* Danquah, Meri
    Nana-Ama;
    Intermarriage; Liu, Eric;
    Melting Pot.
Australia, 178

Barber, Benjamin, 55. *See also
    Jihad vs. McWorld.*
Bavaria, 182
Belief, religious: and
    individualism, 79
Benedict, Ruth. *See Patterns
    of Culture.*
Berlin, Isaiah, 173; on Herder,
    161–162; on nationalism,
    156–157
Biculturalism. *See
    Multiculturalism.*
Bilingual Education Act
    (1968), 52
Biological determinism, 36

Birthrates, 112
Black Americans, 8, 159; and
    racial bias, 9, 116–117
Bloom, Allan, 131
Boas, Franz. *See Anthropology
    and Modern Life.*
Brazil, 33
Britain, 5, 8, 102, 182
Bulworth (film), 117
Bureaucracy, 129
Burke, Edmund, 161, 163

California, 114
Canada, 26, 33, 55–57, 60, 165;
    and defense of cultures,
    61–62; and
    multiculturalism, 15,
    60–62, 157–158, 159; and
    national identity, 102–103;
    and the U.S., 62, 158–159.
    See also Nunavut;
    Quebec.
Carter, Jimmy, 195 n7
Catholics, Roman, 79, 91
Caucasus, 179, 181
Caws, Peter, 80, 95, 98
CBS News, 182
Celebration, Florida, 16
Census, 47, 53, 54; and
    American Indians, 67–68

Index

Index

Index

Index

A NOTE ON THE AUTHOR

Christopher Clausen was born in Richmond, Virginia, and educated at Earlham College, the University of Chicago, and Queen's University in Canada, where he received a Ph.D. He has written widely on literature (especially poetry) and culture. In addition to poems which have appeared in a number of literary reviews, he has written *The Place of Poetry, The Moral Imagination,* and *My Life with President Kennedy.* He is professor of English at The Pennsylvania State University.